AF255228

"After thirty-five years in ministry, I can say without hesitation that I've never seen pastors in crisis like I'm observing right now. I'm thankful that pastor Josh Taylor has written this book. It's helpful in ways that bring the biblical and the practical together, both for the pastor and his family as well as the congregation itself. I hope you will benefit from the insights Taylor shares in these pages."

—**Clayton King**, pastor and overseer, Newspring Church

"In *A Preach Well Church*, pastor Josh Taylor blends transparent testimony and careful research to expose challenges that confront pastors and lead to ministerial burnout. Taylor shares from his personal experience in ministry as well as survey responses from other pastors. While painting an accurate picture of the obstacles, Taylor avoids defeatist hopelessness by offering practical tips for churches and pastors."

—**Kristopher K. Barnett**, associate dean, Clamp Divinity School, Anderson University

"The ministry of the Word is an intersection of heaven and earth, for God places the treasures of his glory in jars of clay. Sadly, churches often expect heaven on earth from their ministers. In this much-needed book, Josh Taylor draws from a wealth of research to offer seven practical ways to support preachers in the work of ministry 'that they may do it with joy, and not with grief: for that is unprofitable for you' (Heb 13:17)."

—**Joel R. Beeke**, president, Puritan Reformed Theological Seminary

A Preach Well Church

A Preach Well Church

How Churches Can Stop Burning Out Pastors

JOSH TAYLOR

WIPF *&* STOCK · Eugene, Oregon

To Mandy, Scotty, Haddon, and Baby Peanut

Contents

Illustrations

Acknowledgments

THIS BOOK WOULD NOT have been possible without the incomparable sacrifices of my wife, Amanda, and my children, Scottlynn and Haddon, as well as the unceasing support of my Mom, Dad, family, and in-laws. My heartfelt appreciation goes out to Nathan and Elizabeth Mobley for their contribution toward the editing of this book, Jo and Marty Evans for their generous hospitality, Rev. Brian Williams for his example of faithful preaching, and Dr. Sidharth Patel and Rev. Chris Huff for their help through my difficult time with panic attacks.

The works of Rae Jean Proeschold-Bell and Archibald D. Hart were essential to this book's foundation. Rev. Tim Dowdy reviewed the Preach Well Survey. Georgia Baptist Associational Mission Strategists assisted in the distribution of it. Above all, I am greatly indebted to the Georgia Southern Baptist pastors who participated in the Preach Well Survey.

Dr. Michael Duduit and the faculty of the Clamp Divinity School who instruct in the Doctor of Ministry in Biblical Preaching program were extremely helpful. Dr. Kristopher Barnett honed the subject, gave words to many initial ideas, and refined the research methodology. Without Dr. Chuck Fuller's imagination and insistence, there would be no proposal for a Preach Well Church, and my cohort was more encouraging to me than I deserved.

I thank God for my church, Mt. Carmel Baptist Church, who is the embodiment of a Preach Well Church. My secretary, Cindy Pruitt, and my deacons serve exceptionally well so that I can preach well. I am also indebted to my Forge group's prayers, which brought this book to fruition. I offer this book to my Savior and God, Jesus, who bled and died for me. May this book make much of him.

Preach Well,

Josh Taylor

1

Introduction: Panic Attacks
and Preaching

"The anxieties which we feel in connection with our pulpit
work are enough to make us old before our time."
—CHARLES SPURGEON[1]

PASTOR ANDREW AND HIS wife have decided to resign from their
ministry because of the stress and toxicity that has come with it.
They have endured gossip and outright lies to malign their charac-
ter. Despite seeing fruit in their ministry, it has become untenable,
and their family is facing joblessness and homelessness.

Pastor Bruce's church is facing financial disaster. The church
has been hemorrhaging money for months, and the account is on
track to be completely dry by the end of the month. Pastor Bruce is
terrified of what this means for his church and family.

Pastor Charles's church is growing rapidly, and he is struggling to keep up. He is working long hours, and his stress levels
are through the roof. One day, he collapses from exhaustion and is
hospitalized. His doctor tells him that if he doesn't take some time
to relax he is at risk of having a heart attack.

Pastor Dan is under a great deal of stress. He is guiding his
church through changes and updates. The church asked him to
make these updates, but the congregation is not always willing to

---

1. Spurgeon, "Burden of the Word."

follow through with these changes. Pastor Dan is trying to balance the church's needs with the congregation's wishes.

Pastor Edward is working hard to revitalize a church that has been struggling due to a drop in attendance. After all their revitalization efforts, the church decides to close. Pastor Edward and his wife have been offered positions outside the church and are in the process of transitioning.

These are just a few examples of real-life pastors in crisis, but they are not unique. Many more pastors are reluctant to open up about their struggles. Pastors all around the country are struggling to keep their churches alive. Many churches face closure, and their pastors feel overwhelmed and stressed to their breaking point.

Many things make it challenging to be a pastor. We are constantly confronted by our sins, pleading for God's mercy to make us sufficient for his call on our lives. We take on the burden of other people's issues. We feel their pain. We wrestle with their questions. We try to help them through their problems. We want to help everyone, but we cannot. When we do not measure up to others' expectations, we feel discouraged. We hate to disappoint our people. When we're not reaching people, we feel like we're not doing enough. We are pulled in many directions. We have families at home that need our attention, a church going through hardship, and personal issues we are dealing with all at the same time. Sometimes, it feels like the whole world is against us. We are fighting an uphill battle. If you're a pastor, this book is for you; more importantly, if you're a church member who loves their pastor, this book is for you!

The Problem

A special issue of *Mental Health, Religion and Culture* provided examples of research on how work-related psychological health, stress, and burnout can affect clergy. The magazine had six empirical articles and five book reviews based on research among clergy in Australia, the United Kingdom, and the United States. The study found that clergy burnout is a common problem, no matter what religious denomination or country the clergy are from.[2]

Clergy shoulder a heavy burden. From providing grief counseling to officiating funerals, clergy willingly take on the challenging task of supporting people through life's most difficult moments. Nearly one-quarter of all people in the United States seek help from clergy for help with mental illnesses.[3] Clergy often negotiate tricky situations, such as what role the church should play in the surrounding community and how to spend limited church funds. Those communities around churches vary. Some communities are doing well and growing, while others seem to be dying. Such situations do not seem to have right or wrong answers, exposing clergy to criticism. Within a single congregation, church members may have differing views on how to proceed, making it impossible for clergy to satisfy everyone. And on top of all that, church members often have different expectations of the pastor's family.[4]

In 2014, 1 in 4 pastors admitted they have struggled with mental illness. Half of those pastors said the illness had been diagnosed.[5] Stress has been a big problem for Southern Baptist ministers especially. In 2002, the number one and number two medications prescribed for Southern Baptist ministers were for stress-related diseases.[6]

Burnout

According to the International Classification of Diseases, burnout is now a legitimate medical diagnosis in the World Health Organization's handbook. According to the manual, a doctor may diagnose someone with burnout if they exhibit the following symptoms: feelings of energy depletion or exhaustion, increased

---

2. Lewis et al., "Clergy Work-Related Psychological Health," 1–8.

3. Proeschold-Bell et al., "Glory of God," 705.

4. Proeschold-Bell et al., "Glory of God," 705.

5. "Acute Mental Illness."

6. Hawkins, *High Calling High Anxiety*, 49–50.

mental distance from one's job, negativism or cynicism related to one's job career, and reduced professional efficacy.[7] In terms of "people work," burnout is a "syndrome of emotional exhaustion, depersonalization, and reduced personal accomplishment that can occur among individuals who do people work of some kind." It results from the long-term emotional stress that one experiences from dealing extensively with people regularly. Burnout has also been called compassion fatigue.[8]

Burnout occurs more often in vocations in which helping people is the primary focus.[9] Pastors are susceptible to burnout because they are frequently in direct contact with people's needs. Over a long span of time, the pastor, who was once brimming with passion, initiative-taking, inspiring others to service, suddenly finds himself reduced to an ineffective and useless state. He gradually becomes isolated and depressed, remaining in bed and hiding in secret. Pastors can become overextended, over-engaged, and altogether overburdened by the emotional demands that others place upon them. The greater the number of people a pastor feels responsible for, the greater the risk of burnout.

The Priority of Preaching

Why write a book about burnout among pastors and discuss preaching? In one of my first pastoral ministries undergraduate classes, I had a professor ask the class to list the top ten things a pastor should do. Our classes' collective list looked something like this, in no particular order:

1. Administration

2. Visitation

3. Evangelism

4. Discipleship

---

7. Prior, "Burnout Is an Official."
8. Hart, "Depressed, Stressed, and Burned Out," 22.
9. Hart, "Depressed, Stressed, and Burned Out," 27.

5. Counseling

6. Sermon Preparation

7. Preaching

8. Worship Services

9. Contacting Visitors

10. Meetings

I gave little thought to it. I guess I considered them all equally important, but the biblical reality is this: they are not. Notably absent was prayer—a sadly overlooked priority of pastors.

Good stewardship of a pastor's time and energy should not be measured by what they do but rather by what they focus on. Too many pastors overextend themselves and succumb to burnout because they can't say no to good things. And, equally too often, a relentless schedule filled with good things distracts us and leaves little room for our biblical primary responsibility: preaching and praying. Throughout this book, I will show how Scripture commands that preaching and praying be the pastor's priority. This is not just good advice—it is God's commandment. Preaching and prayer are Christ's priority for pastoral ministry. These responsibilities should be championed above any other task within a pastor's role. If we're going to burn out, let's commit ourselves to burning out in the pulpit and on our knees.

Another way of looking at this is instead of trying to rank a pastor's many duties into which are more important than the other, its more fitting to conceptualize them like a solar system with planets orbiting around a sun. Preaching and praying are the sun. The importance of these two fundamental roles does not imply that all other responsibilities become insignificant or unnecessary. Instead, they become secondary in the sense that they orbit around and derive their place from preaching and praying. Pastors will take on different roles at particular times, depending on each context, but pastors must build their ministries around this core calling: praying and preaching. Make no mistake: to sacrifice preaching and prayer with some other pastoral duty would represent an abdication of the biblical view of the pastorate. All other responsibilities circle around this.

The New Testament repeatedly teaches that a pastor is responsible for preaching the word. As to the priority of preaching in the pastor's ministry, the apostle Paul charges young pastor Timothy in 2 Tim 4:1–2 to preach the word with five preceding intensifiers. "I solemnly exhort you in the presence of God and of Christ Jesus, who is to judge the living and the dead, and by his appearing and his kingdom: preach the word; be ready in season and out of season; correct, rebuke, and exhort, with great patience and instruction" (2 Tim 4:1–2). John Piper writes, "There is nothing quite like it anywhere else in Scripture. . . . I am not aware of any other biblical command that has such an extended, exalted, intensifying introduction." He continues, "I doubt that anyone has ever overstated the seriousness that Paul is seeking to awaken here."[10]

To be this kind of pastor, you must devote a significant amount of time and effort every week to faithfully complete the task, but once the realities of overseeing a church kick in, pastors scramble to devote time to preaching and prayer. On top of that, many church members have been under-discipled as to preaching's importance. While some church members won't outright say it, many want their pastors to operate like successful CEOs or hospital chaplains rather than preachers of God's Word. "Of course," they say, "it goes without saying that preaching is important." Still, that sentiment betrays that preaching has been overshadowed by something more important, and leading and instructing a church about the priority of preaching is not an easy endeavor. To keep preaching the priority in the pastor's ministry will mean significantly shifting the way things have always been done for most church members. It will be exceedingly difficult for the pastor who wants to impart this biblical vision and shepherd them in this old but new way of church life.

10. Piper, *Expository Exultation*, 66.

The Sweet Torture of Sunday Morning

The prince of preachers, Charles Spurgeon, stated in a sermon, "I do not know what you think about sermons; you imagine preaching is straightforward work. It is not so for me."[11] The regular preaching of God's word to God's flock is a sacred trust that demands the utmost devotion. Even preaching can rapidly become a "burdensome joy," as James Earl Massey dubbed it.[12] In an interview titled "The Sweet Torture of Sunday Morning," Gardner C. Taylor said, "There is a sense, of course, in which preaching is an albatross on all of us. I go through a dreadful time on Sunday mornings getting ready to preach. Sometimes I pass laborers on my way to church and wish I were doing anything except having to come over here and get into that pulpit again."[13] Massey also describes the burden of preaching as "an inward pressure—indeed, as a distress."[14] He says that this feeling can be caused by many things, like our fears or doubts about our abilities, not being able to accomplish what we want, failure, or our creative juices running dry. All of these fears can make pastors want to give up![15]

In an interview, when asked how preaching had affected him personally, Haddon Robinson responded, "There are all kinds of things happening in me that would shock the people in the pew if they knew. The trumpet doesn't give an uncertain sound, but there are times when a trumpeter is uncertain." Inevitably, pastors come to the place when they think, "'Who am I to preach this?' That clouds your life." Robinson related how his wife could easily ruin him on almost any given Sunday if she just asked him when he got home from preaching, "How committed are you? Is that really true about you?" Robinson answers, "Yes, it is true. But not totally true. I can easily be made to feel like a hypocrite."[16]

11. Spurgeon, "Dire Disease Strangely Cured," 286.

12. Massey, *Burdensome Joy of Preaching*, 13.

13. Muck and Robbins, "Sweet Torture of Sunday Morning."

14. Massey, *Burdensome Joy of Preaching*, 14.

15. Massey, *Burdensome Joy of Preaching*, 20.

16. "Pulpit's Personal Side."

On the first page in the preface of his little book *The Person in the Pulpit*, Willard F. Jabusch writes:

> Sometimes preachers get discouraged, not so much because of worries concerning content or technique—as important as these are—but rather because of who we are. For preaching has a way of revealing our personal weaknesses. We tend to get weary, drained of physical and mental energy; we feel the weight of a weekly obligation. We feel guilty about our superficiality, glib and banal words, our lack of prayer and preparation. But most of all, in our most honest moments, we know we are really not worthy of such a role in the Christian community.[17]

Henry Baker Adams, professor of pastoral theology at Yale Divinity School, explains that it is fitting for pastors to experience exceptional stress. It is audacious to speak on behalf of the Almighty. He maintains that the pastor should spend much time meditating on what it entails to stand behind the sacred desk. Talk of sufficiency betrays one's lack of appreciation for the high responsibility and heavy burden of preaching. The prophets depended upon God to sustain them because, ultimately, preaching is supernatural. Only divinely-given capacities can accomplish the task.[18]

The Essential Stress of Preaching

Hans Selye, the father of stress research, defined stress as "the nonspecific response of the body to any demand."[19] Based on this definition, no one can avoid stress. Donald H. Weiss observes in *Managing Stress*, "When something happens, we react to it. Stress is a part of our interpretation of the events in our situation. Only the dead cannot react to the world around them or inside themselves."[20] Not all so-called "stressors" are inherently bad stress. The human body reacts in the same manner to any stress,

17. Jabusch, *Person in the Pulpit*, 9.

18. Adams, *Preaching*, 83.

19. Hart, "Depressed, Stressed, And Burned Out," 23.

20. Weiss, *Managing Stress*, 1.

good (eustress) or bad (distress). The excitement of preaching a sermon can be as stressful as confronting an upset church member after a church business meeting. Both eustress and distress place similar demands on the human body and can wreak havoc.

So, experiencing stress related to preaching does not mean there is something wrong with the pastor. Not experiencing stress at all would seem more questionable. There is an essential stress to preaching. The hours that pastors put into praying and preparing a sermon strain the mind and the body. They wrestle with honest questions regarding the text and the discrepancies they perceive in their own lives. Pastors pour themselves out, pleading with listeners to repent of their sins and wholeheartedly entrust themselves to Christ. Often, no one seems to change. It's also not unusual for fatigue to set in after the adrenaline rush of preaching. There are reasons pastors talk about the "Monday blues."

A Shared Burden

So, why write to church members about a pastor's problem? One of the first lessons that my pastor growing up passed along to me, from a long line of sage advice from pastors, was this: this calling is the best because of the people, and this calling is the worst because of the people. My contention is that pastoral burnout is a shared problem, so it requires a shared solution. It's time to recognize that pastoral burnout is a church problem. The best remedy lies in a collective effort. It will require the love and sacrifice of those within the church to overcome it.

Pastors are often surrounded by people, but that does not mean they receive support from them. Besides other pastors, few people understand the isolation of the pastorate. One survey found that 23 percent of pastors "sometimes get the social and emotional support [they] need," while 6 percent "rarely" or "never" get it.[21] When pastors do reach out to others for help to cope with ministry demands, they usually speak to their spouses.

21. Proeschold-Bell and Byassee, *Faithful and Fractured*, 128.

Research participants were asked, "What relationships have been most significant in supporting and empowering your preaching ministry?" The most significant support comes from the pastor's relationship with his wife (see figure 1).

What relationships have been most significant in supporting and empowering your preaching ministry?

Figure 1. Most Significant Supportive Relationship.

Research participants also were asked, "How do you evaluate your sermon?" A pastor asks his wife for feedback on the message (see figure 2).

How do you evaluate your sermon?

Figure 2. Sermon Evaluation.

Confiding in and sharing emotions with someone makes you feel less lonely and stressed. This is often helpful, even if you don't get any new ideas or observations.[22] Sadly, some pastors do not feel comfortable talking about their problems with other pastors in their local associations and state conventions because they feel like there is too much competition between them. In addition, pastors sometimes feel it is risky to be transparent with church members. Even if they take the plunge and are rewarded with a reliable friendship with a fellow church member, it often doesn't last long because people move to other churches or communities. However, pastors must not face stress alone.

When a pastor exhibits symptoms of burnout, it is often difficult for local churches to address the issue gently and frankly. Church members perceive "something is off" with the pastor. He

22. Proeschold-Bell and Byassee, *Faithful and Fractured*, 68.

is different from what he used to be, but they cannot pin down the cause. Most churches want their pastors to be successful, but they don't always know how to help. The church may choose to look the other way, hoping it will resolve on its own. Churches too easily end up with patterns of behavior that make it harder for the pulpit and the pew.[23] All the while, the pastor may be unaware of the problem, too embarrassed to address it, or does not know how to approach the church about it. Churches can fix this by setting reasonable minimal commitments to help create a "Preach Well" church.

Commitments of a Preach Well Church

A Preach Well Church is a church whose concern for the overall well-being of their pastor reflects their priority for the preaching of the word. Each chapter in this book is a commitment developed from research to help churches help their pastors preach well. Each commitment has clear, concrete actions that pastors and churches can prayerfully consider to create a church culture conducive to keeping preaching as the priority of the pastor's ministry. The following commitments should be tailored to fit a specific church's unique context, purpose, and financial ability.

Also included in each chapter is "A Word to Pastors." No matter your job or who you are, you will experience stress. Pastors can do some things to help them not feel as stressed before, during, and after preaching. Those who address the following problems are more likely to become better pastors and preachers.

The Research

I reviewed the written works and stories of historical and contemporary homileticians and pastors who shared their firsthand experiences with stress related to pastoral ministry and preaching. Based on this literary research, I designed an online survey

23. Keck, *Healthy Churches, Faithful Pastors*, 99.

and distributed it to Georgia Southern Baptist pastors. I adapted the survey questions from portions of older vocational clergy surveys and asked them about their preaching, stress, and coping mechanisms. At the end of the survey, I asked them if they were willing to answer some more open-ended questions about their personal experience with stress.

The research study looked at ninety-seven Georgia Southern Baptist pastors. The pastors were chosen because they are responsible for preaching regularly. The study focused on senior pastors, including "solo" pastors. These pastors usually preach at least once a week to the same congregation. This limitation was put in place to focus on how preaching affects the stress of the pastor who preaches weekly to the same people.

These Georgia Southern Baptist pastors were a reasonably homogenous group. Ninety-eight percent were male. Eighty-two percent were older than forty-five years old. Ninety-three percent were white. Ninety-seven percent were married. Eighty-three percent completed some degree of higher education. Sixty-eight percent were from a rural setting. Twenty-three percent served as a bi-vocational minister (employed as a pastor and in another job outside of ministry), and 53 percent served as a full-time employee (forty or more hours per week) by a church. Forty-four percent served as a senior pastor (other ministry roles on staff), and 39 percent served as a solo pastor (only pastor on staff). Still, the results may well apply to pastors of other congregationally-governed churches and possibly to other denominations.

My Story

In the spring of 2012, I was newly married, working as a full-time associate pastor, and enrolled in a full load of classes in my first graduate semester. Crippling panic attacks began to control my life. I had never heard of panic attacks, but they are debilitating. I remember some of the irrational thoughts that swirled in my mind. I was stuck in imagining the worst was going to happen, like getting food poisoning at a restaurant, getting into a car accident, or getting sick in the pulpit. I felt like my wife was my only safe person. If I went anywhere beyond home and work, she had to be by my side. I read and quoted Scripture, but my anxiety did not stop. I had thought and felt myself into a rut, and my body was past the point of a change of heart and mind immediately reversing the consequences.

It finally came to a head on a Sunday morning. My tightly-held composure finally gave way. I could not preach. My heart was beating out of my chest, and panic took over. I felt like I was losing control. Afraid of how the panic might distract the church during the worship service, I retreated to my office. There a friend and my senior pastor were waiting for me. I explained what was happening. My senior pastor stepped into the pulpit for me, sent me home, and suggested that I see a doctor. It became clear that significant life changes needed to be made. I needed to rest and pay attention to my mental health.

I visited my family physician for help. I told him that there must be something wrong with my heart. He strapped an EKG on me and showed me. There was nothing wrong with my heart. I was experiencing textbook definition panic attacks, symptomatic of generalized anxiety and panic disorder. Ongoing, unaddressed panic attacks often leave people with an anxiety disorder: stuck in a perpetual cycle of staying alert in case of further panic attacks, which induces more panic attacks.

My panic attacks were like a menacing shark dwelling in the ocean, waiting for the opportunity to strike. With prolonged stress, it rises from the depths. It creeps up, swimming just under the surface of the waters. Then, it breaches and wreaks havoc on its unsuspecting victim. Despite initially feeling powerless against this creature, I eventually realized that there were some things I could do to reduce the stress and return it to the depths.

My doctor prescribed two medications to treat my anxiety, each addressing a different issue. One medication was an SSRI, a selective serotonin reuptake inhibitor. Serotonin is correlated to mental well-being. An SSRI blocks your brain from reabsorbing all the serotonin, leaving a reservoir of serotonin to maintain levels for future stress. The other medication was a minor tranquilizer to relieve panic attacks.

For some Christians, considering the role of medications for mental well-being poses a problem. Though I do not present the following as medical advice, I am persuaded that mental health is affected by both spiritual and physical factors. The relationship between mind and body is analogous to Mozart sitting behind an out-of-tune piano. No amount of talent can make up for an instrument that needs adjustment. Conversely, I could sit behind a brand-new baby grand piano, but its excellency will not make up for my lack of skill. Similarly, mental health issues can be caused by complex interactions between body and soul. A holistic approach that addresses both the physical brain and the spiritual mind is necessary for effective treatment and healing—an integration of spiritual practices rather than relying on psychological or physiological approaches alone.

The doctor forewarned me that I could experience some side effects through the first two to three weeks, and then it would ease up, and I would feel in control. Sleep was now possible. I feel like I slept for two weeks. One time, I came in from work, leaned forward into a recliner with my knees in the seat and my face in the back of the chair, and immediately fell asleep. Little by little, each good night's rest restored balance until, eventually, something changed. One day, I felt like my old self. I could sense myself regaining control over my mental health. Anxiousness would pop up every now and then, but it was nothing compared to how it affected me.

Per the doctor, the medications were biding my time to address the sources of my long-term stress. Through professional help and much reflection, I identified some personal variables that probably precipitated my panic attacks and several coping mechanisms that have helped with my stress. In the fall of 2012, my doctor took me off one of my medications due to the progress he observed. Today, I am no longer on any medication. I believe the Lord used this experience to awaken a curiosity in me for researching how pastors and churches can address stress and burnout in ministry. This book is the result of that curiosity and research. Stress and burnout among pastors is an all too common reality. Empty preachers are filling pulpits. What can churches and pastors do to preach well?

Summary

Clergy burnout studies have consistently shown that clergy members feel a lot of stress, no matter their denomination or country. Pastors can feel burdened by preaching. Nevertheless, preaching should be the priority of the pastor's ministry. This book aims to encourage pastors and show church members the incredible weight of delivering God's word and to equip them with practices they can commit to in order to help their pastors preach well. In the next chapter, churches are challenged to take "The Control Commitment" and let go of control over their pastor's schedule.

2

The Control Commitment

*"Pastoral work is hard work, often a night and
day occupation, weighed down with anxiety
and tears."* —T. E. WILSON[1]

IN THE INITIAL MONTHS of the lockdown of the COVID-19 pandemic, as a pastor myself, I prerecorded Sunday's sermon in advance, usually in the late hours of Thursday night into the wee hours of Friday morning. This gave me plenty of time for editing and uploading to our server for streaming live on Sunday morning. When Sunday morning came, I would still get up for church and head to my office to watch the service there. At the time, I did not trust my internet service, and I felt that I could best troubleshoot any problems my church may experience with the live stream from my office. Unbeknownst to me, I wasn't the only person still headed to my church, even though we were not gathering.

One Sunday, as the live stream was ending, I heard a knock on my office door. I was startled. I hollered my usual, "One second!" As the final seconds of the live stream came to an end. I rolled my chair over to the door, opened it, and to my surprise, it was Brother Ricky. Brother Ricky is something of a staple at my church. He had voluntarily led the worship music for years. There he stood, socially distancing himself six feet away from me inside my secretary's office, which is adjacent to mine. "Brother Ricky!" I

---

1. Charles, "Crash Course."

shouted. He was one of the first members of my church I had physically seen since the lockdown. I asked what he was doing here. He shared with me that he and his wife still got up many Sundays and came to the church parking lot to watch the live stream. He just needed to be there. He finally couldn't resist coming inside to fellowship with his pastor and offer me words of encouragement—classic Ricky. As he talked to me, tears began to swell in his eyes. He sincerely appreciated my efforts to keep preaching the word to Christ's church in whatever capacity I could. After he prayed for me, he asked, "So, what's next?" I said, "Well, we do it all over again." I will never forget the look on his face. The simplicity of my answer struck him. "Yeah, I guess you're right," he said as he nodded in agreement. "We do it all over again." As Pastor H. B. Charles has said, "Preaching should be gloriously monotonous. You don't need new truth when you have the same Christ."[2]

Halford E. Luccock, professor of homiletics at Yale Divinity School, likens preaching on a regular basis to Sisyphus. Sisyphus was sentenced to pushing a boulder up a steep slope for all eternity, only to have it roll back down again and again and again. Once you've prepared a sermon and delivered it, it's time to do it all over again. Preaching becomes a well-worn path. Today may seem so much like the same day a week before. Preaching regularly leaves us feeling like we've duped ourselves![3]

I once heard a comedian tell a joke about how his mom wished for him to go to a Christian college and become a pastor. The comedian made light of the situation. As far as he was concerned, he said that if he did, he would be doing the same thing he's doing now . . . but on Sunday. It's amusing, but we laugh because it is a tragically accurate portrait of the state of preaching. However, there is a distinction worth mentioning. With each show, comedians have the chance to perfect the same material in front of a new audience. Every week, pastors try to prepare fresh sermons and deliver them, usually, to the same group of people again.

2. "'He Must Increase' Continues."

3. Luccock, *In the Minister's Workshop*, 33.

A pastor must find new ways to say the same things over and over again—elementary truths which have not taken hold, much less bore fruit. With the preacher of old, we cry, "Vanity! Vanity! All is vanity!" The pastor is constantly fighting a war of attrition, for preaching demands all the energy one can wring from his flesh. The repeated effort continually wears him down. It is something the novice must be ready to meet. Pastors grow tired and weary. They question their effectiveness. They live with much hindsight. They long to preach carefree but not surrender their true concern for their flock. Preaching burns up their spirit; the constant hammering and refining must yield gold or break it. Now add into the mix of the never-done work of preaching: COVID-19.

COVID Decision Fatigue

Pastors have been thinking about quitting their job a lot lately. In 2021, 38 percent of Protestant pastors said they had thought about quitting. This was up from 29 percent, or nearly a third more, when Barna first asked the question in January of that year.[4] This may be because of COVID-19. The last few years have been really hard on pastors and their mental health. Isolation from quarantine led to a historically high rate of depression, anxiety, addiction, and abuse. Chuck DeGroat, professor of counseling and Christian spirituality at Western Theological Seminary in Holland, Michigan, notes that pastors are tasked with the responsibility of mediating differences in church doctrine and practice, such as women's role in church leadership or the recent "worship wars." The pandemic and deep political divides have only added additional pressures on pastors.[5]

Church members were willing to abandon their churches over such issues as church closures and mask policies. Whatever decision they made, pastors were bound to make someone upset, and some pastors even described that they were suffering from

---

4. "38% of U.S. Pastors."

5. Smietana, "For Some Pastors."

"decision fatigue." In addition, it's no secret that the immediate demand for streaming church services left many pastors dumbfounded. Pastors were overworked because of the pandemic and desperately need time off. Is it any wonder that many pastors contemplated resigning amid the pandemic?[6] If your pastor endured, they likely have a genuine calling to serve your church, so give your pastor some grace. It wasn't easy.

The Stressful, Out-of-Control Nature of Spurgeon's Ministry

Even without a roaring pandemic, as mentioned previously, there is an essential stress in ministry. The apostle Paul confessed as much in 2 Cor 11:28: "Apart from such external things, there is the daily pressure on me of concern for all the churches." There is also an essential stress in preaching. John Stott, a theologian and celebrated preacher, stated unequivocally that his favorite verses for preachers were 1 Cor 2:1–5, where Paul comes to Corinth "in weakness and fear, and in great trembling." Nevertheless, Paul's anxiety did not thwart his ministry. His philosophy regarding burdensome ministry could be summed up with 2 Cor 12:15: "I will most gladly spend and be expended for your souls."

No one may have better understood this concept than the prince of preachers, Charles Spurgeon. He noted that to plead for souls, see them deny Christ, face the pressures of overseeing the church, and see the saints stumble are all heavy burdens to bear.[7] It came to a head for Spurgeon on the evening of October 19, 1856, at the Music Hall of Royal Surrey Gardens. Just a month before, the Spurgeons welcomed two sons into the world, and Spurgeon's popularity had forced his church to rent out the Music Hall. A vast number, some estimate seven thousand or more, assembled to hear Spurgeon preach. As he prayed before preaching, some bad actor shouted, and panic ensued. There was a rush to the doors, and

6. Chandler, "Pastors Express 'Decision Fatigue.'"

7. Spurgeon, *Lectures to My Students*, 161.

seven people were trampled to death. Twenty-eight were seriously injured.[8] When Spurgeon realized what had happened, he had to be led from the pulpit. Church leaders observed how this incident adversely affected the "nervous system of our pastor."[9] Spurgeon thought he would never preach again: "It might well seem that the ministry which promised to be so largely influential was silenced for ever."[10] As a result, he canceled several preaching engagements and missed a Sunday in the pulpit. When he returned, he opened with this prayer: "We are assembled here, O Lord, this day, with mingled feelings of joy and sorrow—Thy servant feared that he should never be able to meet this congregation again."[11]

When contemplating the awesome responsibility of preaching the gospel, Spurgeon recalled, "My deacons know well enough how, when I first preached in Exeter Hall, there was scarcely ever an occasion, in which they left me alone for ten minutes before the service, but they would find me in a most fearful state of sickness, produced by that tremendous thought of my solemn responsibility."[12] Spurgeon later remarked, "I have preached the gospel now these thirty years and more, and some of you will scarcely believe it, but in my vestry behind that door, before I come to address the congregation in this Tabernacle, I tremble like an aspen leaf; and often, in coming down to this pulpit, have I felt my knees knock together."[13]

Spurgeon gave his students a remarkable lecture on his depression, titled "The Minister's Fainting Fits." In it, he said, "I thought it might be consolatory to some of my brethren if I gave my thoughts thereon, that younger men might not fancy that some strange thing had happened to them when they became for a season possessed by melancholy; and that sadder men might

8. Nettles, *Living by Revealed Truth*, loc. 2396.

9. Nettles, *Living by Revealed Truth*, loc. 2396.

10. Spurgeon et al., *Autobiography of Charles H. Spurgeon*, loc. 10572.

11. Spurgeon el al., *Autobiography of Charles H. Spurgeon*, loc. 10680.

12. Spurgeon, "Removal," 619.

13. Spurgeon, "Sermon of Personal Testimony," 296.

know that one upon whom the sun has shone right joyously did not always walk in the light."[14]

Spurgeon claims that preaching was painful for him for many years because of his fears before entering the pulpit. His dread of facing the congregation was overwhelming. The stress made him sick. He wrote about it to his grandfather, who was also a preacher. His grandfather wrote back, "I have been preaching for sixty years, and I still feel many tremblings. Be content to have it so, for when your emotion goes away, your strength will be gone."[15]

Spurgeon argues that some pastors are too strong to be strengthened by the Lord, and so "his preaching is like a painted fire; no one is cheered or alarmed by it."[16] He believed that an overwhelming sense of weakness should not be despised; instead, pastors should readily and always rely upon Christ to sustain them. If a pastor knows nothing of the headache and heartache of preaching, he should not expect to have a ministry that extends beyond his lifetime. There is nothing wrong with finding balance, exercising, eating healthy, and getting a good night's sleep, but to depend upon them alone for a Christ-exalting ministry is precarious. "A prophet of the Lord without a burden is an unprofitable servant and a burden to the church." It is a dreadful thing to be a pastor without stress. Pastors should not envy the pastor who can always go to bed without any restlessness. No pastor should ever say preaching is easy.[17]

Spurgeon asks, "Can the Spirit of God, even the Infinite Deity, ride in such frail chariots as these [preachers], without straining the axle, and making the whole machine to quiver, as if it would be utterly dissolved beneath its sacred burden?"[18] When God uses a pastor with soul-saving force, it is consuming. Nevertheless, pastors must humbly welcome such holy fires. They must be either

14. Spurgeon, *Lectures to My Students*, 154.

15. Spurgeon, *Lectures to My Students*, 170.

16. Spurgeon, *All-Round Ministry*, 170.

17. Spurgeon, *All-Round Ministry*, 172.

18. Spurgeon, *All-Round Ministry*, 146–47.

devoured by their corruptions or consumed by their zeal for God. They were made for this purpose. They cannot ignore it.

Yet Spurgeon also understood that the stress of preaching could be taken too far. Pastors may feel their responsibility so profoundly that they can feel no joy. Spurgeon admonishes, "Do not take an exaggerated view of what the Lord expects of you. He will not blame you for not doing beyond your mental power or physical strength. You must be faithful, but you are not bound to be successful."[19] He tells his students, "We are not the Father, nor the Savior, nor the Comforter."[20]

Often, this pressure comes from the pastor himself. Spurgeon asks again, "What is the practical result of making yourself, as one man, responsible for the work of twenty men? Will you do any-more?" The Lord does not treat his pastors this way. Pastors over-load themselves. They strain as if the world's salvation depended upon their saving arm, yet they cannot stand in the place of God.[21]

The Control Commitment: Relinquish Control of Your Pastor's Schedule

Acknowledge that, due to the nature of ministry, the pastor's work cannot be rigidly regulated.

Other times, this pressure comes from the church herself. Church members' misconceptions about what it takes to preach exacerbate problems for pastors. Michael Fabarez notes that a pastor's sched-ule is often out of sync with his congregation's. As their week winds down, his winds up.[22] Compounding the problem is the mystery of a flexible schedule. The pastor may be at the store in the afternoon instead of the office, yet he will be at the church that evening until

19. Spurgeon, *All-Round Ministry*, 175.
20. Spurgeon, *All-Round Ministry*, 175.
21. Spurgeon, *All-Round Ministry*, 176.
22. Fabarez, *Preaching that Changes Lives*, 84.

10:00. This is sometimes misunderstood since many church members serve in non-flexible work environments.

The pastor's flexible schedule is both good and bad. It is good because it lets the pastor do his work while still having some personal time, but it is bad because people might get the wrong idea about what the pastor is doing. Some church members think their pastor spends his whole week chatting, reading books for fun, and playing golf. But in reality, the pastor spends most of his week studying intensely so he can preach on Sundays.[23]

Another aspect of the pastor's schedule is a twenty-four-hour shift. The church may call on him for emergencies at all hours of the night and day. Sometimes what is not an emergency to one church member is to another. How to respond to emergencies is not always obvious. One wants a visit; another wants their privacy. All the while, the pastor is never far removed from the next sermon. Few church members realize the time and energy necessary to become an effective preacher. At the same time, many of them want to receive the pastor's attention because he is an effective preacher. Note how an effective preacher creates only an increased demand for his time. Nevertheless, the pastor cannot be at every church member's beck and call. Emergencies happen and will disrupt the pastor's schedule—and rightfully so. Diversions are part of the ministry, and so God's will, and pastors honor that. However, these should be extraordinary—not the norm—and should not require that he forever forgoes rest.

Spurgeon noted, "Our Sabbath [Sunday] is our day of toil, and if we do not rest upon some other day, we shall break down." Spurgeon himself kept Wednesday as his day of rest as often as he could.[24] A pastor's rest must be made up some other time, so church members must relinquish control of their pastor's schedule. If churches cannot trust pastors with their time, they should not trust them with God's word.

23. Fabarez, *Preaching that Changes Lives*, 84.

24. Piper, *Brothers, We Are Not Professionals*, 188.

A Word to Pastors

Pastor, you are responsible for sticking to your schedule. You cannot constantly be reacting to every conceivable need for which you are not biblically responsible. Still, there is a way you can create a buffer in your schedule for emergencies. Jay Adams suggests that pastors plan out six months of sermons in advance. Now I'm not saying six months of full-fledged sermon manuscripts; that would be impossible! I'm talking about a plan. Take a day and sit down with a calendar of six months of preaching opportunities and fill in potential scripture texts and subjects, big ideas and questions, titles and headings, points and sub-points, and outlines and summaries for each opportunity. I encourage you to plan series of sermons on particular books of the Bible. That way, you can preach the first sermon in light of the whole series. Planning in advance also reduces preaching your "pet topic." Planning requires you to think about presenting a balanced diet to the flock.[25]

I know some are saying, "But what about the Holy Spirit? Aren't you removing him from the sermon process?" I have a couple of responses to that objection. The Holy Spirit can use planning just as he can use spontaneity. He is a God of order and control. Also, no one is saying if the Holy Spirit leads you to deliver a different sermon than the one you have planned that you should grieve him and stick to the plan!

After you plan out your six months of sermons, as you go about your week, study, meditate, and try to gain perspective on the upcoming sermons. As Adams notes, "Too many sermons are cut down green; they do not have time to ripen." Planning your preaching gives your sermons time to ripen. For instance, pastors know how difficult it can be to find an excellent illustration, but when you plan your preaching, illustrations can come naturally. When pastors know what they will be preaching, all the general reading they do and their experiences feed into their upcoming sermons. Pastors who plan don't have to search for sermon illustrations; they come to them.

25. Adams, *Preaching with Purpose*, 80–81.

If I could recommend only one book for pastors to read about this exercise, it's Stephen Rummage's "Planning Your Preaching." Rummage considers ten spiritual and practical advantages for creating a plan for your preaching. I want to emphasize three of them.

One, planning saves time. Many pastors lament that they lack the time necessary to fulfill their responsibilities. Trying to pick what to preach each week is a significant time-waster. "What am I going to preach on Sunday?" is a typical Monday morning question for pastors. Rummage exclaims, "Only one thing is worse than sitting at your desk on Monday and not knowing what to preach Sunday, and that is sitting at your desk on Saturday and not knowing what to preach Sunday!" Pastors who have a plan save themselves the stress and time it takes to figure out what to preach next. When those pastors sit down on Monday, they already know what they'll be preaching on Sunday and the Sunday after that.[26]

Two, planning saves time for interruptions and emergencies. There are weeks when something unexpected happens, like a funeral or many hospital visits, and pastors need to take some time away from sermon preparation. That's part of the ministry! If they plan well, they can spread out their preparation over several weeks so that hectic weeks don't impact their preaching too much.[27]

Three, planning reduces stress. When pastors are under the pressure of preparing a sermon, they can't spend quality time with their families. The thought of unfinished work consumes their mind during their family time. However, if you have a plan in place, you can take a break from studying and focus on your family. It's a pleasure, not a burden, to take a break from sermon preparation since it's all been arranged in advance.[28]

26. Rummage, *Planning Your Preaching*, loc. 196–206.

27. Rummage, *Planning Your Preaching*, loc. 206–11.

28. Rummage, *Planning Your Preaching*, loc. 235–40.

Summary

Pastors will become tired and weary because their work is un-predictable. If their church understands this and is supportive, church members will release control of their pastor's schedule. Pastors can also feel less stressed about hectic weeks if they plan their sermons months in advance. In the next chapter, pastors and churches are advised to take "The Expectations Commitment" and agree on a set of expectations so that both parties know what is important to each other.

3

The Expectations Commitment

"I have never once feared the devil, but I tremble
every time I enter the pulpit." —John Knox[1]

Seth Godin writes, "It's comforting to use someone else's priorities to guide our work. It lets us off the hook, but the only way to do our best work is to realize that part of what it means to do our work is to own the priorities as well. Your boat, your compass."[2] Prioritizing is like mapping a territory. A map is not a picture. Certain features are intentionally left out to ease navigation. The same goes for prioritizing pastoral tasks. It's not so much that tasks are eliminated, but the pastor must choose which features are in the background or in the foreground. Without pastors making this conscious decision and owning it themselves, pastoring remains a wilderness.

Many church members hope the pastor can get everything done equally well. This is impossible, and pastors will have to choose what they will focus on. The pastor has to prioritize what he does and explain to church members why he is doing it that way. It can be hard for the pastor to do this because sometimes church members have unrealistic expectations of him. Sometimes, a church's unrealistic expectations of the pastor are due to church members themselves, but other times, it's due to the pastor. The pastor does not understand his role from the Bible well or quickly

1. Buice, "Legacy of Faithfulness: John Knox."
2. Godin, "Priorities."

changes his priorities when church members make complaints. Pastors must keep preaching as the priority of their ministry, and church members must help the pastor preach well.[3]

The Pastor's Biblical Priorities

Without a biblical understanding of pastoral ministry, the pastor agonizes over meeting an infinite number of illusive expectations. In *Preaching with Purpose: The Urgent Task of Homiletics*, Jay E. Adams cuts to the quick in that often pastors do tasks that don't belong to them, ignoring the plain teaching of Eph 4:11–12, which states, "for the equipping of the saints for the work of ministry." When pastors claim for themselves roles that other believers should and could be fulfilling, pastors make it easy for believers to avoid their God-given responsibilities. They also rob believers of the blessing of utilizing their spiritual gifts and crowd out time for sermon preparation. It ought to be the rule of every pastor not to do anything that a member of his church can do as well or better. Of course, pastors must do these things in emergencies and new church plants, but they should not make it a habit. Instead, the pastor should motivate the members of the flock to minister.[4]

While every believer ought to mature in the word so they can teach others (Heb 5:12), few should occupy teaching positions in the church, for it incurs a stricter judgment (Jas 3:1). John Owen emphasized, "The first and principal duty of a pastor is to feed the flock by diligent preaching of the word."[5] A pastor is singularly responsible for preaching. Preaching and sermon preparation are not exclusively all that he does, but they, along with prayer, have the priority. God has set the pastor apart for this purpose. While his ministry is beyond the scope of the pulpit, it is never out from under its shadow. So, the pastor must prioritize the preaching ministry. The needs will never end, but one thing is most needful.

3. Keck, *Healthy Churches, Faithful Pastors*, 121.

4. Adams, *Preaching with Purpose*, 79.

5. Owen, *True Nature*, loc. 1443.

In response to "What else do you think is crucial for us to know regarding your stress as a preacher?" one research participant wrote, "Congregations—no matter what model of governance—need education on this subject so that congregational expectations of the preacher are clear." Pastors should teach their congregations about the priority of preaching.[6] They need to explain from the Bible why it is important. This means that they should also teach from the Bible about what is the pastor's and the church's biblical responsibilities. This will help ensure that both the pastor and the church are on the same page.[7] This way, the church won't impose unfair expectations on the pastor, like expecting him to do all the work without church members' help.[8]

The Equation

Jason K. Allen reminds pastors that while the biblical expectations are high, "the nonbiblical ones held by many churches are higher still. No pastor is omnicompetent, and none can be omnipresent. Yet today's pastor is often expected to be both."[9] Pastors often experience role conflict. Role conflict is when expectations are such that they cannot be fulfilled concurrently. It exists when an individual who is torn by incompatible work demands is asked to do things they don't want to do or is asked to do something they think is not part of their job.

Balancing multiple roles is difficult, and churches need various roles at various times. In *Letters Along the Way*, D. A. Carson and John Woodbridge write, "The modern pastor in America is expected to be a preacher, counselor, administrator, PR guru, fund-raiser and hand-holder. Depending on the size of the church he serves, he may have to be an expert on youth . . . something of an accountant,

---

6. Adams, *Preaching with Purpose*, 59.

7. Adams, *Preaching with Purpose*, 182.

8. Proeschold-Bell and Byassee, *Faithful and Fractured*, 58–59.

9. Allen, *Portraits of a Pastor*, 11.

janitor, evangelist, small groups expert, an excellent chair of committees, a team player, and a transparent leader."[10]

Clergy have concerns about dealing with the unrealistic expectations from church members.[11] "Several factors contribute to unmanageable personal stress, which can also be interpreted as the abuse of self, including . . . unrealistic work expectations by self and others coupled with the difficulty in saying no."[12] Sometimes clergy feel pressured to do what people want, especially if they are donors to the church.[13] They are on call twenty-four hours a day, and these demands from church members can be intrusive to both the clergy and their families.[14] Some congregations even discourage pastors from vacationing when church members are sick in case a funeral is needed.[15] It's hard on pastors when their people are disappointed or angry because their expectations weren't met.[16]

Pastors also experience role ambiguity. Role ambiguity exists when an individual has insufficient information about the work expected of him. This happens a lot in pastoral ministry because each church member has a different idea of what the pastor should be doing. If a church has two hundred members, that's two hundred different ideas about what the pastor should do! And on top of that, church members cannot see everything the pastor does. Much of pastoral ministry is spiritual in nature and can't be seen by other people, like prayer and meditation. People who are not in ministry might not understand what is happening, so it often looks like nothing is getting done.

It can be tough to show church members that what they expect is unrealistic or unbiblical, especially if they are unhappy with the pastor. Most pastors will tell you that they do not want to just please people, but this is not always true. They prefer people

10. Carson and Woodbridge, *Letters Along the Way*, 148.

11. Berry et al., "Ministry and Stress," 165.

12. Birk et al., "Religious Occupations and Stress Questionnaire."

13. Monahan, "Who Controls Church Work," 370.

14. Wells, "Moderating Effects," 873.

15. Proeschold-Bell et al., "Theoretical Model," 700.

16. Keck, *Healthy Churches, Faithful Pastors*, 12.

to affirm them instead of being at odds with them. Pastors enjoy receiving compliments just like everyone else does! It's challenging to deal with criticism from people we think love us, and it's hard to keep our priorities straight when they are different from what our people want. If a pastor is success-oriented and doesn't have a biblical perspective on his role or is very critical of himself, it's only a matter of time before he burns out. Pastoral burnout can be summed up in the following equation: pastoral burnout = church members' unbiblical, unrealistic expectations + a lack of perspective + a penchant for criticism.

The Expectations Commitment: Review Expectations and Priorities for Mutuality

Annually ensure that the agreed-upon expectations and priorities of the pastor are observed and adjusted when required, permitting him to discuss potential problems.

Pastors are accountable to God, yet God does not conduct an annual performance review. Pastors report to their congregations, respective boards, or personnel committees. It is no surprise that pastors who rely on others' opinions may experience lower levels of positive mental health.[17] One research participant states, "The expectations of others—perceived or real—have always been an issue for me. I am a bit of a people pleaser." Pastors aim to please God and not appease others, but every pastor knows that people must at least affirm their call to ministry. Even when people tell a pastor that he "answers to God alone," they do not mean it. No church adopts this thought as its employment philosophy. It would abolish the church's accountability.

The pastors surveyed were also asked how pleased they were with how much importance their congregation attaches to the time their pastor sets aside for sermon preparation. Pastors who were extremely pleased tend to have less stress related to preaching. In

17. Proeschold-Bell et al., "Using Effort-Reward Imbalance Theory," 439.

other words, if pastors are pleased with how much importance their congregation attaches to the time they set aside for sermon preparation, then preaching becomes a less stressful task.

One research participant left a significant response to "What else do you think is crucial for us to know regarding your stress as a preacher?" He writes, "I really don't have a high level of stress. The church I serve doesn't have unrealistic expectations and allows me time to focus on preaching and teaching." This shows how important it is for a pastor to have a supportive congregation. If the congregation isn't supportive, it makes preaching very hard and stressful.

Gary McIntosh and Robert L. Edmonson confess that pastors dream of a church with absolutely no disagreement regarding their performance, but these churches do not exist. This is because church members often have different expectations of their pastor. This should not be surprising, considering the variety of people and backgrounds represented in the average local church.[18] In *Meet Generation Z*, James Emery White writes, "I could tell you there are actually six living generations in America, but I don't want to add to your stress."[19] The diverse problems and perspectives combine to create impossible expectations of a pastor. The pastor cannot function as an administrator, teacher, facilitator, mentor, counselor, and all-around expert on life. The inherent conflicts in these roles are apparent since no pastor has enough hours in the day to do everything. Nevertheless, pastors often face pressure to keep as many people pleased as possible.[20]

Every church member acknowledges that pastors should ignore unrealistic expectations, except when their pastor does it during their time of need. This is when pastors must understand the difference between "rational" and "irrational" guilt. As explained by Brooks R. Faulkner in *Burnout in Ministry*, rational guilt comes from God and helps pastors behave ethically. Pastors need it to conduct themselves in a way that is consistent with their calling. Irrational

18. McIntosh and Edmondson, *It Only Hurts on Monday*, 56.

19. White, *Meet Generation Z*, 37.

20. McIntosh and Edmondson, *It Only Hurts on Monday*, 57.

guilt is the kind of guilt that happens for no ethical reason. It's when other people make us feel guilty not because we did something wrong but because we didn't please them. Faulkner asserts that it is the "ought" trips we "allow" others to impose on us.[21]

Paul Tournier, a Christian doctor from Switzerland, said that guilt can be divided into two types: true guilt (or "value guilt") and false guilt (or "functional guilt"). Tournier says that a feeling of "value guilt" is the genuine consciousness of having betrayed an authentic standard. A feeling of "functional guilt" is when you feel guilty because someone else made you feel guilty or because you are afraid of losing the love of others. Pastors need not go on these guilt trips. Pastors permit them to happen because they feel obligated to these individuals. If making someone feel guilty is part of a church member's behavior, the pastor should have grace for themselves and be able to say no to their demands.[22]

Putting it all together, the church should address the following items with the pastor to help him preach well. First, an understanding should be reached about what the pastor's priorities are. If not, the amount of work would be insurmountable for the pastor and prevent them from having a life outside of the church. Second, pastors should communicate their days off and give advance notice of vacations. Doing so allows lay leaders to divert others from interrupting his time off. Third, when disagreements about expectations between pastors and church members arise, lay leaders should address them immediately with gentleness and respect.

Lay leaders should provide a job description from either a ministerial staff handbook or a church constitution. They should ask their pastor to prayerfully consider and answer each of the following four questions:

- What on here are you alone getting done?

- What on here can you not do?

- What on here is someone helping you do?

21. Faulkner, *Burnout in Ministry*, 77.

22. Faulkner, *Burnout in Ministry*, 78.

- What on here is unrealistic?

Direct dialogue benefits all parties involved, inevitably limiting pastors' work overload, resolving issues, and preventing pastors and church members from experiencing needless harmful feelings.

A Word to Pastors

Pastor, you must discern when to be what and self-impose limits on your ministry. In *Healthy Churches, Faithful Pastors*, David Keck observes, "Given a pastor's tendencies and desires and given those dominant personalities in a congregation who may insist on having a particular type of pastor—one the rest of the congregation may not need—this ongoing work of faithful discernment can be very difficult."[23] That is why D. A. Carson rightly admonishes, "Many of our people expect us to be counselors first, administrators second and thirdly to be preachers. And we're supposed to do that without much study—we learned all of that in seminary, didn't we? Sometimes we fit into this expectation by the sheer dictatorial power of the urgent. . . . Somehow or other as part of our commitment to preaching . . . [we must] draw a line."[24]

Pastoral work is, by nature, unpredictable. One can make it slightly less so by setting boundaries based on biblical priorities. Derek J. Prime and Alistair Begg argue that pastors get the balance right only by determining their priorities and sticking to them as rigidly as they can, without feeling failure if they cannot always do so.[25] They suggest that pastors sit down quietly, in an attitude of prayer, and write down their current priorities and what they ought to do to meet them. This exercise may reveal areas where they have gotten their responsibilities out of balance.[26] Answer this: What kinds of calls should the pastor always respond to personally and

23. Keck, *Healthy Churches, Faithful Pastors*, 55.
24. Fabarez, *Preaching that Changes Lives*, 88.
25. Prime and Begg, *On Being a Pastor*, 273.
26. Prime and Begg, *On Being a Pastor*, 284.

right away? And what might the pastor be able to hand off for a few hours, and to whom? Not all tasks in the pastor's job description can be the top.[27] They are all essential but not weighted equally. Keck suggests reframing the issue in terms of succession by asking, "How can I shepherd the church, so my successor comes into a healthier church?" When a pastor prioritizes ministry needs while considering his successor, he is freed from needing immediate results and can advocate for the church's long-term best interests.[28]

Two-thirds of pastors with low mental health have a hard time saying no. They often do more work than they should.[29] Pastors with positive mental health set boundaries. This includes agreeing to take specific days off each week and taking a vacation every year. They set office hours and let people know they will not be taking calls at a certain time of day. Some pastors create boundaries by not attending certain meetings.[30] People may not like this, but it's the only way to ensure you stay healthy and focus on your family.[31]

One of the critical distinctions between flourishing and low mental health with burnout is having boundaries between the ministry and personal life. A reoccurring theme in Jason K. Allen's *Portraits of a Pastor* is the priority of the pastor's family. Two of the requirements for leading Christ's church are that, if the pastor is married, he must be devoted to his wife, and, if he is a father, he must be dedicated to his children.[32] It should be impossible for a Christian man to be content with half-hearted care for his family and remain a pastor. Christ demands that the pastor's family is prioritized.[33] Pastors betray their family when he disciples others before his children and visits the widow and never dates his wife. One participant, in response to the question "How would you advise pastors to prepare themselves for preaching stress?"

27. Proeschold-Bell and Byassee, *Faithful and Fractured*, 52.

28. Keck, *Healthy Churches, Faithful Pastors*, 82.

29. Proeschold-Bell and Byassee, *Faithful and Fractured*, 137.

30. Proeschold-Bell and Byassee, *Faithful and Fractured*, 134–35.

31. Proeschold-Bell and Byassee, *Faithful and Fractured*, 137.

32. Allen, *Portraits of a Pastor*, 34.

33. Allen, *Portraits of a Pastor*, 39.

answered, "The greatest thing a pastor can do to reduce his stress is to place his family before his ministry."

There are some recommendations from H. B. London for pastors who have church members with unrealistic expectations. The pastor should have at least one distinguished ministry, like preaching or pastoral care. When church members know that the pastor is good at something else, they will overlook some of his other shortcomings. The pastor should maximize his efforts in the areas of his gifting. Another way to deal with unrealistic expectations is to accept that a pastor's work is never done. There will always be unfinished tasks, so he has to prioritize what he does each day.[34]

Pastor, remember you can be faithful to biblical expectations without being in high demand. William Gurnall points out, "We shall never be charged for not doing another's work. . . . God requires no more than faithfulness in our place. We do not find fault with an apple-tree if it be laden with apples, though we can find no figs or grapes growing on it. He is a fruitful tree in God's orchard that brings forth his fruit in his season."[35] Do your work for him whose eyes run to and fro throughout the whole earth.

Summary

Some church members have unrealistic expectations of their pastor. This can lead to a lot of stress for the pastor. Pastors must teach their congregations the biblical priority of preaching and not succumb to every comment or complaint voiced by a church member as a statement of expectation. Churches should sit down with their pastor every year and agree on what is expected of the pastor and the church. If pastors want to avoid this stress, they must set boundaries for themselves and not take on too many roles. In the next chapter, church members are asked to accept "The Appointment Commitment," defending the pastor's sermon preparation time from all unnecessary interruptions.

34. London, *Pastors at Greater Risk*, 78.

35. Gurnall, *Christian in Complete Armour*, loc. 6954–63.

4

The Appointment Commitment

*"Effectiveness in teaching the Bible is purchased
at the price of much study, some of it lonely, all
of it tiring." —*D. A. CARSON[1]

DAVID MATHIS ASKS, "WHAT does a good sermon cost?"[2] It will cost more than you expect. One of the most important aspects of a pastor's responsibility is preparing sermons. It is the key to delivering a biblical message to the congregation week after week. Many church members don't understand the amount of work that goes into preparing a sermon. John Piper has it right: "The Bible, after all, is a book. And books must be read to be understood. And skilled reading means good thinking. There is no getting around it. Reading for a complete understanding is hard mental work. Therefore, the preacher's task involves enormous efforts of thinking week after week, year after year. And either we do it well, or we do it poorly. I am pleading for preachers to embrace this task and do it well."[3]

1. Carson, *For the Love of God*, Jan 7.
2. Mathis, "What Does a Good Sermon."
3. Piper, *Expository Exultation*, 129.

Sermon Preparation

Pastors need a lot of time devoted to sermon preparation each week. Before a pastor can preach a text, the text must be understood and prayerfully meditated upon. The only way to understand the text is to read and study it yourself. Sound reasoning is preceded by excellent reading, and excellent reading is mentally exhausting. Skimming over words or not looking up answers to questions may lead pastors down the wrong interpretive path, for which they take their congregations along. There are no shortcuts to comprehension, conviction, and clarity on Sunday mornings. Fabarez emphasizes that sermon preparation time must be given top priority in the pastor's weekly schedule, for all would agree that the "sermon prepared on Saturday evening reveals an attitude that is unworthy of the work." He adds, "The supremacy of preparation in your weekly schedule must be evident to everyone. Indeed, it must be clear that you are called to preparation—not exclusively, but to a very significant extent."[4]

The problem is that much of the sermon preparation process is invisible to most church members. Churchgoers get the impression that their pastor never works. "The only time he works is on Sundays and Wednesdays."[5] They assume that anyone with a seminary degree and gifting can preach extemporaneously, but this reasoning betrays how many church members do not know the cost of sermon preparation each week. In reality, the invisibility of sermon preparation means that most pastors work more hours than people realize. No church member shows up often enough, nor is he ever able to see the silent hours behind the scenes spent in sermon preparation. The work weeks for most pastors can seem endless because their sermon preparation doesn't end until Sunday morning, and as soon as they deliver the sermon, Sunday morning is already coming around again.[6]

---

4. Fabarez, *Preaching that Changes Lives*, 85.

5. Wilkey, "TBMB Leader Discusses Pastoral Burnout."

6. Rainer, "How Much Time."

Sermon preparation and writing are very similar. In "A Sermon on Keeping Children in School," the great Reformer Martin Luther writes that some people believe a writer's work consists of sitting behind a desk, never having to endure hardship, yet no one has put the shoe on the other foot. Everyone is aware only of their own issues and thinks the other person has it made. Luther concedes that the pen is light. However, the best part of the body (the head), the noblest of the members (the tongue), and the highest faculty (speaking) must come together like never before to write. In other professions, people can sing and joke while working, but the writer cannot. Writing is said to require only three fingers, but it is a contribution of body and soul.[7]

On top of this, many pastors feel they do not have enough time to prepare their sermons. They say it is difficult to find regular, uninterrupted time. Most pastors spend around ten to eighteen hours preparing for a sermon. It is important to remember that this is for only one sermon. Some need to prepare more than one a week. This means that many pastors spend over thirty hours every week on sermon preparation, which accounts for 70 percent of their time.[8] Over a year, the average pastor produces the equivalent of a book.[9] Is it any surprise that it is easier to find pre-written messages?

Depending on the number of sermons they expect to preach, pastors in evangelistic churches will devote thirty hours a week to sermon preparation and take any criticism and blame for any other ministry task underperformed. Pastors know sermon preparation means they will have less time to meet with and visit church members and address administrative needs. However, time in God's word is vital to the church's maturity and growth, and these pastors believe that church members are much more competent than they realize at building up the body of Christ (Eph 4:12).[10]

7. Lehmann and Schultz, *Luther's Works*, 213–57.

8. Rainer, "How Much Time."

9. Knowles, *Folly of Preaching*, 58.

10. Rainer, *High Expectations*, loc. 1642–51.

Adams notes that many pastors enjoy preaching, including hours of sermon preparation. The dissatisfaction about preaching from pastors themselves comes from not "having enough time" to prepare. It is the opportunity that pastors enjoy that is lacking. They want to spend more time studying the word, but other demands prevent them from doing so. Inadequate preparation takes away from the joy of preaching.[11]

The Appointment Commitment: Make an Appointment

Defend the pastor's sermon preparation time
from all unnecessary interruptions.

Research participants were asked, "What is the most stressful part of preaching to you?" The most stressful part of preaching is spending time in the word preparing a sermon (see figure 3).

Figure 3. Most Stressful Part of Preaching.

The open-ended questions yielded another common theme concerning sermon preparation. Research participants were asked, "How have you experienced stress in preparing, delivering, and

11. Adams, *Preaching with Purpose*, 78–79.

evaluating sermons?" Preachers feel stress due to a lack of sermon preparation time (see figure 4).

Figure 4. Experience of Stress in Sermon Preparation.

One of the best gifts church members can give their pastor is uninterrupted time to read, think, and pray. Church members should make an appointment instead of dropping by unannounced. If there is no emergency and they need to talk to their pastor, church members should schedule a meeting with the pastor by making an appointment a week out or consulting the pastor's calendar with the church secretary. It's hard to focus on sermon preparation when people keep coming in and out of the church office. Scheduling an appointment or having a standing appointment on a specific day and time will allow the pastor to plan for it and have undistracted time for the church member and uninterrupted time for sermon preparation.

The Pastor's Study or the Church Office

Pastors need a quiet, peaceful place to prepare sermons. Ironically, that place is often not the church office. Fred Craddock relates what betrays many church members' mistaken assumptions about sermon preparation. He writes, "It would be comforting if such comments were rare, and exaggerated, but the one room in the house of God which, judging by its size, furnishings, and location, is an afterthought, is not the parlor but the pastor's study."[12] Eugene Peterson concurs by saying that naming the "pastor's study" an "office" further secularizes perceptions of pastoral work.[13] The pulpit is not the only sacred desk; the pastor's study desk is equally sacred. Fabarez advocates a name change. "The label of 'office' conjures up a business or administrative atmosphere, while the word 'study' serves as a perpetual reminder to everyone, from your secretary to visitors, that your primary weekly task is sermon preparation."[14]

Many church members feel that the pastor's study is a place where they can stop by unannounced. What many church members don't see is that they may be unintentionally sacrificing benefits for the entire church body by not allowing the pastor to focus on the word. In his seminal work, *The Effective Pastor*, Robert C. Anderson writes, "Because the pulpit represents the pastor's most public appearance and because it is likely that he reaches more people from the pulpit than in any other aspect of his ministry, he should determine to give pulpit ministry the very best he has, or he should leave the pastorate. If he remains a pastor, he should realize the sermon that he preaches on Sunday morning may have a greater impact than anything else he does the entire week."[15] When church members believe they are interrupting the most impactful part of pastoral ministry and not just office hours, they will be more intentional, even prayerful, about making an appointment.

A Word to Pastors

Pastors should use their study as their "Bethel," as G. Campbell Morgan emphasizes. He says, "If you will make your study the place of your nearest approach to God, if you will tarry there until

12. Craddock, *Preaching*, 71.

13. Peterson, *Working the Angles*, loc. 661–63.

14. Fabarez, *Preaching that Changes Lives*, 86.

15. Anderson, *Effective Pastor*, 180.

He gives light . . . if with shut door and open Bible you will wait upon Him, surely He will speak through His Word to you as never before . . . and so anointed will you go forth to preach that men shall be blessed through your message." Every pastor needs a Bethel, a consecrated prayer space amid a busy life. It need not be a holy site, but it should be a location where there will be no intrusions. The pastor's Bethel should be his study. The pastor's study is not just a workroom. The pastor's study should serve as a location where he may seek God's face and talk personally with him.[16]

Keck asks a wise question: "Do you think your congregation views your workspace as the 'Pastor's Study' or the 'Pastor's Office'?" One denotes a place where sustained reading is valued; the other values administration.[17] According to some church members, preparing a sermon in your "office" means you have time to talk for a few minutes . . . or an hour. Pastors know unforeseen circumstances and emergencies will happen and derail the best-laid sermon preparation plans. That's part of ministry, but many pastors find themselves slaves to the next interruption in the church office. Pastors should not sacrifice the spiritual well-being of their entire congregation to accommodate the handful who insist on interrupting their sermon preparation.[18]

If the church office is your primary place of study, being in the church office cannot mean you are accessible to church members on a whim. Pastor, it's up to you to educate your congregation on the demands of sermon preparation. If this is not communicated, then the church office is probably not a good place to prepare your sermon. For this reason, you may want to consider another location to study.

If you want to remain in the study at your church, you may want to establish a practice where church members should schedule an appointment to meet with you. Scheduling an appointment with their pastor will be a challenge for many church members who grew up in a culture where it's appropriate to stop

16. Morgan, *Practice of Prayer*, 109.

17. Keck, *Healthy Churches, Faithful Pastors*, 148.

18. Fabarez, *Preaching that Changes Lives*, 88.

by the pastor's study without an appointment. So, pastors need to be patient as these ideas are implemented. It takes a while for many long-standing church members to calibrate to a pastor's new way of doing things.

To help your congregation embrace scheduling an appointment with you, you will need to communicate and impress upon your congregation the importance of giving you time to prepare your sermon. Pastor, you must be convinced yourself that your preaching and prayer ministry is the most impactful thing you do. McDill agrees: "There is no other aspect of the pastoral work that has as much potential good as preaching. What else does the pastor do in any other half-hour that can affect as many people?"[19]

Peterson asks, "How many pastors no longer come to their desks as places for learning but as operation centers for organizing projects?"[20] Pastors should know that devotion to God's word and prayer is the fountain of their ministry, and they need to disciple their congregation, and especially their lay leaders, about the importance of the work that goes into sermon preparation. Many people believe that sermon preparation is a quick and easy process. By explaining the amount of work that goes into sermon preparation, church members will be more likely to respect their pastor's time and allow him to focus on preparing his messages without interruption.

Another way to help your congregation understand is to have them take part. Appoint a lay leader to preach in your stead when you are sick, on vacation, or simply taking time out of the pulpit. They will better understand how much work goes into sermon preparation and the pressure of preaching to a congregation. It also causes your congregation to depend upon God's word regardless of who is preaching. This will help create an environment where the pastor can focus on preparing his messages without distractions.

Pastor, you must find a balance between time spent in sermon preparation and time spent around your flock. Not only because you need to understand your congregation but also

19. McDill, *12 Essential Skills*, loc. 5102.

20. Peterson, *Working the Angles*, loc. 661–63.

because some time away from sermon preparation can keep you physically and mentally healthy. Sermon preparation is mainly a sedentary activity. Pastors whose work depends upon intellectual and spiritual activity often neglect their physical health, which in turn affects their mental health.

Spurgeon writes, "All mental work tends to weary and to depress, for much study is a weariness of the flesh; but ours is more than mental work—it is heart work, the labor of our inmost soul."[21] In *Lectures to My Students*, Spurgeon instructs young pastors not to neglect the tools of the trade: their bodies. To sit for a long time studying a book or writing with a quill in a poorly ventilated chamber without long periods of rest and loaded with a heavy heart, especially in the damp months of fog, you have the makings of a seething cauldron of depression.[22] Sometimes, we must get up from our study and move around for the sake of our sanity.

Pastor, your sermon preparation time—the time in your study—is a time to draw near God and to resist the devil. Pastors' spiritual adversary desires that they focus more on outward things than spiritual development. Awareness of the presence of God encourages pastors.[23] The last thing the devil wants is for a pastor to spend uninterrupted hours of prayer and meditation in preparation for a sermon and be assured that God is with him. Prime and Begg concur, "While God's presence with us does not depend upon our feelings, the greatest blessing God can give His people is the awareness He is with them."[24] Time and time again throughout the Scriptures, reluctant prophets, except for the notable departure of Jonah, are eager to know if the Lord will go with them.

As the servant of the man of God felt the pressures of the surrounding army, the prophet Elisha prayed for him: "LORD, please, open his eyes so that he may see" (2 Kgs 6:15–20). The Lord opened the servant's eyes and realized his enemies were outnumbered. Norman encourages pastors to learn to pray the following prayer in

---

21. Spurgeon, *Lectures to My Students*, 156.

22. Spurgeon, *Lectures to My Students*, 177.

23. Prime and Begg, *On Being a Pastor*, 95–96.

24. Prime and Begg, *On Being a Pastor*, 201.

the same way: "Lead me in each moment of study. I need to sense your presence at every point in my preparation time."[25] Spurgeon reminds pastors, "In the study, when we sit down and rub our foreheads and anxiously enquire, 'What shall we preach about?' let us turn towards our Lord and pray with our window open towards His cross and His throne. All disciples labor in the Lord's presence." That is not a "pretty piece of romance."[26] The Lord is with us just as much in the study as he is in the pulpit.

As the psalmist David said, "You know when I sit down and when I get up; You understand my thought from far away. You scrutinize my path and my lying down, and are acquainted with all my ways. Even before there is a word on my tongue, behold, Lord, You know it all. You have encircled me behind and in front, and placed Your hand upon me. Such knowledge is too wonderful for me; It is too high, I cannot comprehend it. Where can I go from Your Spirit? Or where can I flee from Your presence?" (Ps 139:2–7). In *The Art of Faithful Preaching*, William Perkins expounds, "The consideration of God's special providence should teach you to think of the presence of God as all-seeing and all-knowing, to seek his help, and also to believe that you are helped in all things, and finally that there is no danger so terrible, but he is able and willing to deliver you from it, when it is fit."[27]

F. B. Meyer states, "In preaching, there are two, not one, in every pulpit."[28] This is true not only of the sacred desk but also of the study desk. The Holy Spirit came to guide Jesus's disciples into all truth, and he gives pastors help in sermon preparation. The pastor is a land, barren and dry. He is empty until he picks up his Bible. As he prays, a mist rolls over the land. In meditation, the wind and rain pick up. Thunderclouds roll as truth and tradition, reason and experience collide and coalesce, and then hot lightning strikes—the moment of clarity, the thunder of crystallization.

25. Norman, *Preacher as Sermon*, 59–60.

26. Spurgeon, *All-Round Ministry*, 306.

27. Perkins, *Art of Faithful Preaching*, loc. 1406–8.

28. Meyer, *Expository Preaching Plans and Methods*, 7.

The presence of the Holy Spirit is the atmosphere in which sermon preparation is conducted. The Holy Spirit superintends over the whole sermon cycle. Because his divine power is in it, the lightning and thunder will come. Pastors may not sense God's Spirit brooding over the waters, but they can trust he is there. As Stott exclaimed, "May God grant us a more constant and more vivid awareness of his presence, to whom all hearts are open and from whom no secrets are hidden!"[29]

Summary

One way to help the pastor focus on sermon preparation is to defend their time from unnecessary interruptions. This includes coming into the office without an appointment, stopping by to chat when the pastor is busy, or calling during the pastor's study time. If you have something important to discuss, try setting up an appointment with the pastor ahead of time. That way, they'll be able to block out some time for you, and you won't be interrupting their sermon preparation. In the next chapter, churches are asked to make "The Honor Commitment" by providing for their pastor and prioritizing his wellness.

29. Stott, *Between Two Worlds*, 338.

5

The Honor Commitment

"I want to read the Bible from Genesis to Revelation without trying to write a sermon. . . . I want to travel and go sit in the back of somebody's church and hear the word of God and not be worried about what time we got to get out for the next crowd." —Rev. Howard-John Wesley[1]

After preaching to a large congregation for thirty years, Rev. Howard-John Wesley took a much-needed sabbatical. When he announced his leave, he gave two main reasons: feeling disconnected from God and physical exhaustion. Many pastors can agree with his sentiment. Pastoring is draining.

The Everyday Pressures of Pastoral Ministry

In a 2015 Lifeway Research study, 13 percent of senior pastors left their churches for reasons other than death or retirement. The pastors reported that some of the challenges included being available around the clock (84 percent), anticipating disputes in their church (80 percent), feeling that their position can be overwhelming at times (54 percent), and often worrying about their family's financial stability (53 percent). Twenty-one percent of the pastors believed that the expectations set by their church were unreasonable. Most of the pastors admitted that they knew it would be hard

1. Bailey, "'I Feel So Distant.'"

when they took the position. Despite this, one in five pastors said the search team who interviewed them for their current position did not accurately describe the church they would be working for. Nevertheless, other issues make the job more difficult. For example, 71 percent of churches do not have a policy allowing their pastor to take a sabbatical. Thirty percent have no document clearly stating what the church expects of its pastor.

When asked why they left a previous church, more than a third of pastors (34 percent) said it was because their family needed a change. One in five people concluded that the church did not accept their method of pastoral work (19 percent). Eighteen percent of pastors mentioned not feeling like they were a good fit and that the church had unrealistic expectations of them. Some pastors were asked to leave the church (18 percent). Some were reassigned (8 percent). Twenty-three percent of the pastors who left churches say they left because of conflict in the church. Church conflict often manifested in severe personal assaults against 34 percent of the pastors. Thirty-eight percent of respondents experienced a dispute with lay leaders, and 31 percent of respondents found themselves in confrontation with a matriarch or patriarch of the church.[2]

The COVID-19 Pandemic

Besides the everyday pressures of pastoral ministry, no pastor was prepared for COVID-19. The pandemic has been brutal on everyone, especially those in the helping professions. Pastors are no exception. For many pastors, the COVID-19 pandemic has been the straw that broke the camel's back. In a recent survey, almost 40 percent of pastors said they had considered quitting in 2021. The added stress of leading a congregation through a global crisis has taken its toll, and many are now struggling with mental and emotional health. After all, they've dealt with everything from canceled services to dwindling congregations. They've had to find new ways

2. Green, "Despite Stresses, Few Pastors."

to connect with their parishioners online or risk losing them altogether. So it's not surprising that so many pastors are struggling. If you're a pastor who is feeling overwhelmed and is considering quitting, please know that you are not alone. Many other pastors feel the same way, but there is hope.[3]

Spiritual Warfare

Underneath all of this is spiritual warfare. The enemy seeks to destroy us, and ministers are often prime targets. The enemy will do anything to devour ministers. They are always plotting to sow lies in our minds so that we may be lured away from the Lord. Take heart, dear pastor; Jesus has overcome. Through Christ, we have the power to overcome all dark forces. We must be alert and aware of the enemy's schemes, and always prepared to take our stand against the enemy's attack. But know you are not alone; the Holy Spirit is there. He will give you the strength to overcome.

The Honor Commitment: Honor the Word by Providing for Your Pastor and Prioritizing His Wellness

The Honor Commitment is a pledge made by church members to encourage the church to annually review financial agreements made with their pastor and insist their pastor take time off each week. Doing things like this will help make sure that pastors are taken care of.

Honor the Word by Providing for Your Pastor

*Annually review the pastor's financial
agreements and time arrangements.*

Some churches have neglected the Bible's clear teaching that a pastor's work, especially preaching and teaching, deserves

3. "38% Of U.S. Pastors."

respect and compensation (1 Tim 5:17–18; Gal 6:6–10). It is accurate to say that Jesus commands Christians to pay pastors a salary for their service (1 Cor 9:13–14) and that pastors should expect a fair wage (1 Cor 9:7–12). A pastor may refuse a salary if he believes receiving such would undermine the gospel in a given context. However, this is the exception rather than the rule, and it is not the church's responsibility to decide when a pastor should not receive a salary because of the gospel. The decision belongs to the pastor (1 Cor 9:13–18). God calls pastors to endure financial hardship, but not because of a negligent or stingy church. Pastors must flee from and fight against the love of money (Titus 1:11; 1 Pet 5:2; 2 Pet 2:14) and provide for their own families. A pastor who does not provide for his family would disqualify himself from the ministry (1 Tim 6:8).

Every year, the church should have personnel and finance committees review the financial agreements made with their pastor. If you are on a church personnel or finance committee, make this an item on your regular annual agenda. Pastors should be given formal permission to communicate their personal and family financial needs. In addition, the church should research comparable salaries to ensure he receives adequate compensation and benefits. It is a win-win for both the pastor and the church. It ensures that the pastors know they have the church's support behind them, and the church can ensure they are not overpaying or underpaying their pastor. This is a simple way to show support and appreciation, and it can make a big difference in the life of a pastor.

If the church is able, the church should establish a minimum $500 line item in the annual budget for the pastor to buy books, commentaries, and Bible software. In addition, the church may agree to set up a scholarship fund to help the pastor pay for continuing education. This will allow the pastor to grow academically without worrying about tuition. It will be an investment in not only the pastor's ministry but also the church as a whole as he learns new ways to better serve the church.

Prioritize Your Pastor's Wellness

Insist that the pastor takes weekly time off and annual vacations to spend on his personal needs and with his family.

Research participants were asked, "What is the most important thing you do to prevent experiencing high levels of exhaustion and stress in your work as a preacher?" The most crucial thing preachers do to prevent high stress levels is to take time each week for prayer and exercise (see figure 5).

Figure 5. Most Important Thing to Prevent High Levels of Stress.

Research participants were also asked: "What have been some challenges and obstacles to remaining healthy as a pastor?" The challenges of remaining healthy as a preacher are balancing time for church and work, being with family, eating healthy, and exercising (see figure 6).

Figure 6. Obstacles to Remaining Healthy as a Pastor.

Again, research participants were asked, "Suppose elevated levels of exhaustion and stress affected you or a fellow pastor adversely; what is the most important way the local church could help?" Churches can support their pastors by giving and encouraging them to take time off, and even making provisions for sabbaticals (see figure 7).

Figure 7. Most Important Way a Local Church Can Help.

There have been several studies that show that most pastors are not healthy. They often have obesity, chronic diseases, and depression, and a lot of clergy don't even realize how bad these conditions can be for them and their work.[4] In a study of United Methodist clergy in Kansas, 77.4 percent of the clergy participants had a body mass index (BMI) that classified them as overweight or obese based on their self-reported weights and heights. Some challenges they said they faced in maintaining a healthy lifestyle were a lack of family time and an unpredictable work schedule.[5] One study found that clergy who experience more stress or work more hours are more likely to be obese. However, American clergy who take one day off each week, have taken a sabbatical, or are in a support group with other clergy are less likely to be obese.[6]

The preaching process from study to pulpit is often not conducive to a physically or mentally healthy lifestyle. Massey relates that Henry Ward Beecher scarcely ever slept on Saturday night because of his anticipation for Sunday's services. Depression often followed his restlessness because he preached without proper sleep. John Angell James did not sleep on Saturday night because he lay awake with uncontrollable apprehensions. His physiological symptoms included depression (worsened by his sleeplessness), irritability, and nervousness.[7]

The people who participated in the research were asked to check all that statements that applied to the following question: "When you deliver your sermon, do you experience any of the following?" The most common symptoms reported were increased perspiration, dry mouth, and tense muscles (see table 1).

4. Proeschold-Bell et al., "Use of a Randomized."
5. Lindholm et al., "Clergy Wellness," 97.
6. "Studies from Louisiana State University."
7. Massey, *Burdensome Joy of Preaching*, 18–19.

Table 1. Stress Symptoms Experienced in Preaching by Percentage

Symptom	Percentage
Increased perspiration	25.77%
Dry mouth	18.56%
Tense muscles	11.34%
Rapid heartbeat	8.25%
Upset stomach	8.25%
Shortness of breath	5.15%
Being out of it	4.12%
A feeling of panic	3.09%
Shaking	3.09%
Nausea	2.06%
Dizziness	1.03%
Quivering voice	1.03%

After the sermon is delivered, the physical recovery isn't immediate. Most pastors feel tired the day after preaching. According to survey participants, 85.25 percent of pastors agreed or strongly agreed with this statement: "Generally, I feel exhausted the day after preaching" (see figure 8).

Figure 8. Post-Adrenaline Depression Experienced by Percentage.

The preaching process is arduous, taxing, and energy-draining. Sundays are not restful for pastors. The preaching hour is stressful on the body, and for the body to rejuvenate after periods of high demands like preaching, it must be followed by periods of low arousal. As Spurgeon noted, after wrestling all night, Jacob walks with a limp; after the triumph on Mt. Carmel, Elijah contemplates suicide; and after getting swept up to the third heaven, Paul is left with a thorn in the flesh. Thus, God intersperses successes with times of gloom so that all continue to depend on his grace.[8]

In *Lectures to My Students*, Spurgeon laments, "How often, on Lord's-day evenings, do we feel as if life were completely washed out of us! After pouring out our souls over our congregations, we feel like empty earthen pitchers which a child might break." Beecher was so anxious about preaching that he retired to bed with a headache after delivering a sermon. He said, "You will, perhaps, be carried over Monday, but by Tuesday, you begin to come down, and you think the earth is not so bright as it formerly seemed. You begin to think that you have mistaken your vocation and that you will turn farmer. There you have gone down as far

8. Spurgeon, *Lectures to My Students*, 156.

as you ought. Some begin to see the blue devils at that point."[9] Matthew Simpson, in his "Lectures on Preaching Delivered to the Students of Yale College," notes, "I believe one reason why so many ministers complain of 'Blue Monday' is, that they have keyed up their system beyond its natural tension, and, the excitement passing away, they are left depressed."[10]

After attending Phillips Brooks's preaching, an intuitive congregant recorded that he felt a peculiar sensation of physical fatigue as he exited the church. It was comparable to the relief following a lengthy but victorious fight. He wondered, "If this so affects me, what must it be to him [Brooks], and how can he bear it all?" The congregant surmised that it must be this strain that finally defeated Brooks. It was more than a job. As no other man could, he was pouring out his strength and thus putting the power of his listeners to the greatest test.[11]

Daniel Spaite studies the physical impact of pastors' stress and writes about how public speaking impacts the physical body. When a public speaker gives a presentation, his neurohormonal systems are involved. This causes hormonal changes that affect the nervous system. Adrenaline and noradrenaline levels increase significantly when speaking in public. When studies examined the effects of stress on inexperienced and experienced speakers, they found a hormonal alteration in both groups.[12] Essentially, a pastor's body is going to key up to some degree whether it is their first time preaching or ten-thousandth time preaching.

Many pastors wake up Monday mornings to a fog about their heads. Some call it the Monday morning blues.[13] I call it "The Holy Hangover." Pastors whose most physical activity occurs during the weekends can suffer from reduced effectiveness on Mondays and Tuesdays. They are more irritable, more easily upset, and more pessimistic about anything. While adrenaline is up, a pastor is

9. Beecher, *Popular Lectures*, 161.

10. Simpson, "Lectures on Preaching," 44.

11. Capps, *Young Clergy*, 66.

12. Spaite and Goodwin, *Time Bomb in the Church*, 108.

13. Hart, *Unmasking Male Depression*, 42.

protected from the painful consequences of stress. When adrenaline drops, a pastor feels the adverse effects of stress.

Archibald D. Hart calls this phenomenon "post-adrenaline depression."[14] He says, "The clearest and most common manifestation of post-adrenaline depression occurs for pastors on Mondays, following a weekend of preaching and high demand."[15] When you are stressed, whether good or bad, your adrenal glands work hard to help the body stay awake and keep making energy. When the demand is high, like on a Sunday for pastors, the adrenal glands push themselves to produce adrenaline and cortisol; but when the demand drops, like on a Sunday evening, the adrenal system comes crashing down. This can make you feel tired, cranky, and sad. It's vital that you give your adrenal system time to recover so you can feel better.

In this post-adrenaline depression, pastors experience the following symptoms of moderate adrenaline fatigue:

- Occasional muscle tension, resulting in a sore neck, shoulders, and back, and common tension headaches.

- Occasional insomnia, where it is difficult to get to sleep, or one awakens early and cannot get back to sleep.

- Disturbance of the digestive system, resulting in diarrhea, colitis, diverticulitis, ulcers, or constipation.

- Feelings of fatigue—especially waking up tired in the morning.

- Loss of enthusiasm for a job or hobbies, or lack of excitement or interest in usual activities.

- Spiritual lethargy—a feeling of boredom with the church, other Christians, and even God.

- Low-grade feeling of being down, moody, or even slightly depressed.

- Irritability toward spouses, kids, or friends.

14. Hart, *Unmasking Male Depression*, 109.
15. Hart, *Unmasking Male Depression*, 110.

- Looking for something exciting to do—e.g., buying something to feel better.[16]

Hart says the symptoms are typical of withdrawal in several substance addictions. Pastors may have a form of adrenaline addiction from preaching. In a success-driven culture, the church may have unintentionally incentivized this adrenaline addiction. "He is very dedicated to his job!" Or "he hasn't taken a vacation in years!"[17] But after Sunday, the high from the adrenaline drops. They can feel withdrawal symptoms, and the pastor feels like quitting.[18] If your pastor feels overwhelmed or overworked, encourage him to take a break.

A Word to Pastors

Pastor, when you are feeling down after Sunday, it is possible that you are just experiencing post-adrenaline depression. This happens because your body needs time to recover from the stress of working so hard. It is normal for pastors to feel this way sometimes. The symptoms are deliberate. The mood slows one down so healing can occur. Losing interest keeps the body still so the adrenal system can rest. Instead of pushing through, cooperate with your post-adrenaline depression by slowing down and not trying to force yourself to feel better. This will help your body heal and restore itself.[19]

Hart says a pastor may need two days for recovery; however, the time can be cut in half if one cooperates with recovery. A proper response can reduce both the intensity of the depression and the time needed for recovery.[20] Research participants were asked, "What do you do when you feel flat after preaching?" When pastors feel flat, they try to get away, rest, nap, pray, and

16. Hart, *Unmasking Male Depression*, 113–14.

17. Hart, *Unmasking Male Depression*, 117.

18. Hart, *Unmasking Male Depression*, 47.

19. Hart, *Unmasking Male Depression*, 120–21.

20. Hart, *Unmasking Male Depression*, 122–24.

read God's word; however, they often feel compelled to return to work (see figure 9).

Figure 9. What to Do When Feeling Flat after Preaching.

Hart makes some suggestions for dealing with post-adrenaline depression:

- Do not take Monday off. Instead, use it for low-arousal, routine activities tackling no major task while the adrenal system is recovering. Then, take off a day later in the week.

- Accept the feeling of depression as a normal part of the recovery process; it has no other meaning. Do not read into or interpret the feeling or give credence to the pessimistic self-talk that may accompany it.

- Focus on better sleeping habits and a more relaxed lifestyle that prioritizes recovery and recreation.[21]

21. Hart, *Unmasking Male Depression*, 121–24.

Summary

The ministry consumes those who love Jesus and his people. Someone warned Charles Spurgeon, "You will break your constitution down with preaching ten times a week." Spurgeon responded, "Well, if I have done so, I am glad of it. I would do the same again. If I had fifty constitutions I would rejoice to break them down in the service of the Lord Jesus Christ." Spurgeon died at a young age, but not before he had preached nearly 3,600 sermons. Pastoring is a demanding vocation that requires every ounce of energy and focus. And yet, for all its demands, there is no greater joy than to be found proclaiming the gospel week in and week out. Church members can alleviate these demands by encouraging appropriate committees to annually review financial agreements with their pastor and insist that their pastor takes weekly time off and annual vacations to spend on personal and family needs. In the next chapter, church members are charged to take "The Volunteer Commitment," to serve one another with their spiritual gifts.

6

The Volunteer Commitment

*"Take the time we are living in. What discouraging days they are, so discouraging that even a man with an open Bible which he believes, and with the Spirit in him, may at times be discouraged and cast down almost to the depths of despair." —*D. MARTYN LLOYD-JONES[1]

PASTORS PERENNIALLY LAMENT THE culture of their day. In his classic *Between Two Worlds*, John Stott addresses the main impediments to preaching in his day. The anti-authoritarian mood, TV addiction, and culture of skepticism prevent people from listening, effectively silencing preachers. Some preachers give up because of the crises they are facing. Those who continue lack enthusiasm. Even though preachers started countering bad arguments, people have been too affected by negative ones.[2]

In *The Anatomy of Preaching*, David Larsen argues that shifts in community life have made being a pastor more difficult today than thirty years ago. The congregation today views the pastor in light of the preacher on TV. In the post-millennial age, pastors should expect a much fiercer rivalry, a more diverse congregation, and a proliferation of different preaching options because of societal affluence.[3]

1. Lloyd-Jones, *Preaching and Preachers*, 129.

2. Stott, *Between Two Worlds*, 89.

3. Larsen, *Anatomy of Preaching*, 49.

In *Christians in the Age of Outrage*, Ed Stetzer points out that pastors spend hours studying God's word and then fielding questions from individuals with little more than their own opinions. In today's culture, many people ignore facts, logic, and others' arguments just to make their point. Today's outrage emphasizes aggression over accuracy. Controversial yet confident yelling personalities have a large following, even if what they say is incorrect. Pastors live in a time when being wrong is possible but rare. Truth becomes devalued as this attitude permeates society, and public discourse grows complex.[4]

In *Preaching Truth in the Age of Alternative Facts*, William Brosend writes, "How are we to proclaim good news in the era of fake news? How are we to persuade others of the truth of the gospel when we live in a post-truth age? This is a challenge for which few preachers are prepared. And the strain is showing."[5]

In *Meet Generation Z*, James Emery White writes that in a survey by the Pew Research Center of thirty-five thousand Americans, 23 percent of American adults identified as "nones," having no religious affiliation. The "dones," those who were once in the church and have left, make up about 19 percent. The children and youth of these adults, Generation Z, will be the first post-Christian generation. The challenge for pastors is understanding this generation, evangelizing them, and transforming culture.[6]

Declining Attendance and Volunteerism

Pastors today are faced with an issue that has been prevalent in churches for years: low levels of commitment and attendance, but a major plot twist has taken place. Part of this problem was exacerbated by the COVID-19 pandemic when many of our very own churches began streaming their sermons. As these churches streamed their sermons online, it gave many the notion that they

4. Stetzer, *Christians in the Age*, 59.

5. Brosend, *Preaching Truth*, loc. 48.

6. White, *Meet Generation Z*, 11–12.

could do away with physical attendance. In doing so, the consumer church culture came full circle; the lowest-common-denominator church shortcutted itself! Why go when you could just sit on your couch or in your office chair while listening live to not just any pastor anywhere in the world but your very own pastor!

But there are no shortcuts in discipleship. As churches lower the bar for church members, it is no surprise that we find ourselves becoming less and less committed. Pastors must remind their church members, as Thomas Long notes, that a sermon is more than a lecture delivered in a vacuum.[7] The preaching that God wants you to receive is from a local church elder whom you submit to for accountability and who keeps watch over your soul. This kind of preaching takes place in a specific place among a particular group of people for which you must be present. While biblical truths transcend time and place, God has called and led a particular pastor to you!

Another one of the most pressing issues pastors face today is that volunteerism and service among members have been declining or inconsistent for years. It's hard to find people who will serve, leaving pastors often relying on those same volunteers again and again. This can be frustrating and even discouraging. The pastor can't do it all alone. They need the help of committed volunteers willing to serve in various capacities. Whether it's leading a small group, teaching Sunday School, or helping with the children's ministry, there are many ways that volunteers can make a difference. When church members commit to volunteering, they are committing to ministering to one another and building up the body of Christ.

Compounding the problem are church members who refuse to be ministered by someone who is not the pastor. They may feel that only the pastor can meet their needs, but this is a very limiting perspective. The pastor wasn't given to meet your needs. He was given to the ministry of the word and prayer for you. God gave you a church! The pastor cannot meet the needs of everyone

7. Long, *Witness of Preaching*, 28.

in the church, but there are many other members of the church who can minister to others.

The Volunteer Commitment: Embrace Church Members Discipling and Visiting

Affirm the pastor's biblical freedom to delegate ministry to capable church members.

Pastors are overwhelmed, but there is hope! By taking the volunteer commitment, you pledge to minister to others and be ministered to by others. When you volunteer, you say you care about the church and its members. By serving in your church and receiving ministry from capable church members, the church will become more loving and effective, and you will ease the burden on your pastor. It will go a long, long way.

When it comes to ministry, preaching and discipling are indispensable. They share many of the same objectives: teaching believers biblical doctrine and praxis and equipping them for the work of the ministry. They are two sides of the same coin. Their distinguishing features concern their respective context. Preaching is often more monological in nature and public in scope. Discipling is often more dialogical and limited to professing believers. The Lord Jesus exhibited both shades of instruction, especially with his parables. The Lord often taught his parables publicly to the crowds, then explained the meaning of his parables to his disciples in private. These distinguishing features are advantageous. Preaching is for all people. Discipling allows for more time to give a more thorough explanation and answer questions from the committed. A pastor may feel more at ease presenting a prepared sermon aimed for public hearing. Another pastor may enjoy exploring a subject with others and its vulnerability.

Visitation is another indispensable task in ministry. Visitation of church members including the sick and shut-ins may contribute to pastoral stress because of demands on time. Sermon preparation requires uninterrupted spans of time. Even when visitation is due to a medical emergency or death, it breaks up the flow of sermon preparation, and those affected may call for many hours of visitation or repeated visits during the episode.

Nevertheless, the pastor should not prioritize discipling or visitation over preaching and preparation because discipling and visitation are shared responsibilities of the church. In the New Testament, all disciples are responsible for discipling (Matt 28:18–21); all sheep are responsible for visiting (Matt 25:31–46), and even when the sick call upon the church's leaders for prayer, it is a plurality of elders who do so (Jas 1:27; 5:14–16). This is not to begin a discussion on church governance but to emphasize that the Bible does not envision the pastor as primarily responsible for discipling and visitation. In his book, *Visit the Sick*, Brian Croft concedes, "The ministry of the care and visitation of the sick is not limited to pastors and leaders in the church but is the calling of all. . . . Like the early church's dedication to providing for the needs of the church (Acts 2; 4), we must see this as the calling and responsibility of all members of a local church to one another."[8] The pastor leads the church in fulfilling these commands, not by doing these all by himself. If no other church members share in the church's responsibility to disciple and visit, the pastor must address it.

Limiting visitation for the sake of sermon preparation may become contentious for a local church that has never been taught the biblical precedent for it. In Acts 6, as the early church grew and ministry expanded, certain widows were mistakenly overlooked in the daily distribution of resources. The complaint quickly came to the apostles. The apostles did not malign the early church's vigorous charity. They knew it was needful, but one thing was more needful for them.

The apostles were faced with a tempting decision: put down the ministry of the word and wait on tables or come up with another solution. The former would constitute failure to their Master. The latter required Spirit-inspired ingenuity. Guided by the Holy Spirit, the apostles approached the church with instruction and a solution. The ministry of the word was their specific responsibility. Other

8. Croft, *Visit the Sick*, 14.

early church members were free to assist in the ministry to the widows. This ministry to widows did not have to be carried out by the apostles. Other Spirit-filled leaders could be appointed to do it. The early church saw these changes as appropriate. Michael J. Quicke notes that "the priority of preaching needed to be safeguarded as pastoral pressures built in the new church in Jerusalem."[9] Pastors are not equal to apostles, but pastors have been entrusted with the apostles' word. The apostles set the precedent that pastors should preach and pray more than anything else.[10]

Lloyd-Jones recognizes Acts 6 as establishing the pre-eminence of prayer and preaching in the pastorate. "There, the priorities are laid down once and for ever. This is the primary task of the church, the primary task of the leaders of the church, the people who are set in this position of authority, and we must allow nothing to deflect us from this, however good the cause, however great the need."[11] Again, he writes, "It seems to me to indicate that preaching always comes first and is given priority."[12] Stott warns about what this precedent entails. "If we established 'the ministry of the Word and prayer as our priority, as the apostles did (Acts 6:4), it would involve for most of us a radical restructuring of our programme and timetable, including a considerable delegation of other responsibilities to lay leaders, but it would express a truly New Testament conviction about the essential nature of the pastorate."[13]

Leonard Ravenhill was a British evangelist who challenged western evangelicalism in the mid-twentieth century to evaluate its current state with the early church recorded in the book of Acts. His challenge to pastors still holds true today. Ravenhill tells a story about Alexander Maclaren, who made it very clear what his church could expect from him by asking this question to his deacons before taking the pastorate position: "Gentlemen,

---

9. Quicke, *360-Degree Preaching*, loc. 172–73.

10. Prime and Begg, *On Being a Pastor*, 21.

11. Lloyd-Jones, *Preaching and Preachers*, 30.

12. Lloyd-Jones, *Preaching and Preachers*, 39.

13. Stott, *Between Two Worlds*, 124–25.

there is one matter to settle before I take this position. Do you want my head or my feet? You can have one or the other, not both. I can run around doing this and that and drinking tea, if you wish me to; but don't expect me to bring you something that will shake this city." This question still speaks volumes today as so many pastors are spread too thin between their various duties. For Ravenhill, God does not call men into the pulpit to become jacks-of-all-trades. Instead, pastors' chief biblical duty is to adhere to the requirements of Acts 6 by giving themselves continually to the ministry of the word and prayer.[14]

If the pastor has all ministerial responsibilities but little time for sermon preparation, he has misunderstood the biblical vision of the church. Both pastors and churches of every generation must relearn this Spirit-inspired lesson of Acts 6. Once a pastor has rediscovered this biblical vision of the church as the body of Christ, he will look for ways to empower church members to minister.

Visitation Guidelines

To prevent disputes, pastors should teach and train their congregations what to expect out of a pastoral visit, that church members are expected to visit, and especially that church members will be visited by other church members. Pastors should state to the congregation who the recipients of a pastoral visit are and what the procedure, purposes, and scope of a ministerial visit is. Pastors should prayerfully consider using the following guidelines:

- Pastors should prioritize visitation of formal church members without a Christian family.

In local autonomous Baptist churches, there is no way to identify who is a part of a particular pastor's flock without formal church membership. Church membership is a Christian taking responsibility for a specific church and a church taking responsibility for a specific Christian. A Christian who expects

---

14. Ravenhill, *America Is Too Young*, 38–39.

a pastoral visit should only receive such within the context of covenant church membership. In addition, Christian families are the primary caregivers of those in need. This eases the burdens on the church (1 Tim 5:3–8).

- Church members, if possible, should call the church and request a visit or prayer (Jas 5:14–16).

As a pastor, being aware of the health of your congregation is not an easy task. Some church members just assume we must be aware of their illnesses. Without reliable communication, we are put in the difficult position of meeting expectations that are unrealistic: you can't care if you don't know. Urge church members to take initiative in communicating their illnesses with you. Remind them regularly of your desire to be made aware, informed, and updated. It can pave the way for meaningful pastoral care.[15]

- A ministerial visit is spiritual.

Remember you are a pastor! We are spiritual caregivers. It is essential to integrate spiritual practices into their medical treatment. We have a responsibility to read passages of the Bible to them and pray for their healing. Doing so offers guidance, hope, and strength. Show them the power that comes from relying on God in suffering and sickness.[16] The greatest comfort a pastor or church member can give to any member of the flock is to pray for them and assure them of what God has promised in his word: His presence, forgiveness of sin, bodily resurrection, and eternal life.

- A pastoral visit should stay within the range of ten to thirty minutes.

Crafting meaningful interactions with sick church members is an invaluable skill. On calls to sick church members, pastors must be sensitive in determining the ideal visit length. As Croft asserts, "We actually care for them more faithfully by not pushing the line

15. Hiscox and Hoadley, *Star Book for Ministers*, 22.

16. Hiscox and Hoadley, *Star Book for Ministers*, 23.

and staying too long."[17] Sometimes, a brief call will be all that is desired; other times, an extended face-to-face conversation may be best. Show your compassion by taking the time to understand individual preferences. Your sensitivity will be highly valued![18]

A Word to Pastors

Pastor, if you are living from crisis to crisis, you must learn to prioritize and delegate tasks to associates or lay leaders and rely upon the congregation to meet other members' needs.[19] The correlation between delegation and stress levels is clear: the less a pastor delegates, the more he experiences pastoral stress. When a pastor delegates more, he experiences reduced stress. Pastors feel overwhelmed due to an inability or reluctance to delegate. Pastors must delegate biblically shared responsibilities for much-needed relief to lighten the pastoral load.

Aligning weekly and daily tasks to follow the things most critical for our pastoral calling is essential. Some ministers are so busy that they do not know whether their accomplishments are more driven by other people's priorities or their own. Ministers who manage by crisis merely complete tasks others press on them as urgent rather than the essential things God calls them to do.[20] Saying no without a feeling of guilt is an art in preaching.

In *The 7 Habits of Highly Effective People*, Stephen Covey created a four-quadrant grid to help people prioritize what matters most to them.[21] Covey defines "urgent" as a task requiring immediate attention and "important" as something that contributes to mission, values, and prioritized goals.

Quadrant 1 holds "important and urgent" issues. This includes pressing problems, deadline-driven projects, emergency

17. Croft, *Visit the Sick*, 41.

18. Hiscox and Hoadley, *Star Book for Ministers*, 21.

19. Wilson and Hoffmann, *Preventing Ministry Failure*, 176.

20. Wilson and Hoffmann, *Preventing Ministry Failure*, 149.

21. Covey, *7 Habits*, 159.

meetings, unexpected funerals or hospital visits, misbehaving children, health crises, and intense arguments with spouses. Quadrant 2 holds "important but not urgent" issues. This is where to plan and prepare for the future and work on goals consistent with values, including preparing for sermons, planning family vacations, having lunch with a friend, and taking extended time in personal prayer.[22]

Quadrant 3 holds "not important but urgent" matters, including interruptions, some meetings, some emails, and phone calls, especially those that contradict pastoral calling or conflict with a higher priority. This quadrant is just as crisis-driven as quadrant 1, with one major exception: time. Quadrant 3 is spent on other people's urgent priorities rather than matters consistent with pastoral calling. Quadrant 4 holds "not important and not urgent" issues, including trivial time-wasters, irrelevant emails, phone calls, and things providing a temporary escape from a daily routine (e.g., excessive TV or video games, surfing the internet, nonsensical busywork).[23]

Highly effective people do whatever it takes to focus most of their resources on quadrant 2 issues. Quadrants 1 and 3 compete for time and attention most any day. Quadrant 4 is a waste of time and should be eliminated from a routine by whatever means necessary. Ministers may have more independence in setting their schedules than the average person. Even if that is not true, pastors must ensure they spend adequate time on quadrant 2 activities. Reducing quadrant 1 will require some initial "putting out" of fires. Once extinguished, most will become quadrant 2 priorities. Quadrant 3 is saying "no" to those time demands or delegating them to others. Pastors must take initiative to prioritize quadrant 2 tasks for overall ministry effectiveness.[24]

Once a pastor's biblical priorities are established, he should seek to part with biblically shared responsibilities. Stott argues that even "delegation" is the wrong word, for it suggests that the work is

22. Covey, *7 Habits*, 149.

23. Covey, *7 Habits*, 149.

24. Covey, *7 Habits*, 149–50.

the pastor's, but "partnership" is the more biblical concept. A pastor should lead his church to partner with him in ministry. Some pastors are hesitant to embrace this biblical concept because they equivocate overseeing to being solely responsible for getting the work done. Some churches are uncertain about such an approach to ministry because they have become codependent upon the pastor's presence. Nevertheless, it is the biblical vision.

As Prime and Begg state, "If a job we are doing is not our first priority, and someone else is free and able to do it, we should aim to pass it on."[25] Wherever delegation of other responsibilities is feasible, pastors should practice it. Often, without realizing it, pastors inhibit gifted lay leaders by denying them the opportunity to serve. Overworked pastors and fruitless church members make a toxic combination, and the body of Christ does not mature. When the opposite happens, the entire church glimpses the multifaceted grace of God. "As each one has received a special gift, employ it in serving one another as good stewards of the multifaceted grace of God" (1 Pet 4:10). Healthy churches support pastors by respecting their unique calling, recognizing their distinctive gifts, deficiencies, and imperfections, and accepting their biblically shared responsibilities.[26]

To maximize his time, energy, and resources, the pastor should assemble a team of lay leaders who can work together to care for the church.[27] An excellent way to organize this kind of ministry care is for the pastor to distribute a portion of the church's membership among lay leaders.[28] As Prime and Begg exclaim, "One of the greatest contributions of small groups to the life of the modern church is that they provide a context in which people can give and receive pastoral care without involving the pastor!"[29]

Deacons are to be a tremendous ally to every pastor. The biblical precedent for their responsibility in Acts 6:1–7 is to help church

25. Prime and Begg, *On Being a Pastor*, 240.

26. Keck, *Healthy Churches, Faithful Pastors*, 173.

27. Stott, *Between Two Worlds*, 205–7.

28. Prime and Begg, *On Being a Pastor*, 237.

29. Prime and Begg, *On Being a Pastor*, 155.

leaders by serving as an extension of pastoral care to the congregation. Pastors, equip your deacons with individual lists of sections of the membership of your church. Each deacon can closely track members on their "Congregational Care List" or "Deacon Family." Deacons can provide them with tangible help and support and alert you when special attention is needed, keeping your church family connected and cared for![30]

The good Samaritan cared for the man attacked by robbers and left on the side of the road, and, at the end of the parable, the good Samaritan arranged care for the man. Both are parts of care: giving and arranging. Arranging care is a form of pastoral care. Partner with your deacons in providing care to your church. Adopting this proactive approach to giving pastoral care ensures the entire congregation is being looked after with consideration. When each deacon is responsible for some church members, they can ensure people don't slip through the cracks. With deacons as your partners, pastors are bound to be more effective in seeing that pastoral care is given to the entire congregation!

When asked, "What is the most important thing you do to prevent experiencing high levels of exhaustion and stress?" one research participant wrote, "Delegate! Still learning this one." When pastors answer the question, "What are biblically shared responsibilities?" and prioritize accordingly, they become aware of how many critical tasks will not get done unless another member of the body takes responsibility for it. A pastor's failure to delegate biblically shared responsibilities constitutes an affront to the doctrine of the priesthood of believers. The Holy Spirit indwells and uniquely gifts each believer to benefit the entire body of Christ. God has sovereignly designed his church and provided for her maturity with every member. The pastor can be away from the church, and the church has been well prepared to function without him.[31] Pastors must train their churches as ministers and missionaries, as well as make space for them to solve the church's problems and even make mistakes.

30. Hiscox and Hoadley, *Star Book for Ministers*, 20.

31. Keck, *Healthy Churches, Faithful Pastors*, 27–28.

In an interview, Gardner C. Taylor was reminded that the minister was once called the "parson;" etymologically, he was "the person" in the community. Then Taylor was asked, "Does the preacher feel intimidated by this?" Taylor replied, "He might. But he has to go back to the great universals in which he has authority. Many people are educated, but they are not educated in the Bible as the pastor is. The people before us are dying people who one day will be corpses. A preacher has to assert his uniqueness as a proclaimer of the relationship between the temporal and the eternal."[32] Pastor, prioritize and delegate in such a way to preserve this uniqueness.

Summary

Many church members do not volunteer to minister to one another or refuse to be ministered by someone who is not the pastor. This puts tremendous strain on the pastor. That all can change if you commit to volunteer. You may be hesitant to volunteer. You may think you are too busy with work and other commitments. But it's not a matter of having time, but making time, and you make time for the things that matter. This matters! Your pastor cannot do it alone and needs your help. It will be one of the best decisions you have ever made. Volunteering for a ministry role will be a blessing to you and will build up the church. So serve on a church committee or ministry team, lead a small group or Sunday school class, or participate in outreach events or service projects. Use your gifts and talents to the glory of God! It will bless you, your pastor, and your church!

John Wesley wrote, "Though I am always in haste, I am never in a hurry—because I never undertake any more work than I can go through with perfect calmness of spirit."[33] When a pastor plans their time by understanding what the Bible says about being a pastor, they will be less likely to feel overwhelmed and stressed. This is because

32. Muck and Robbins, "Sweet Torture of Sunday Morning."

33. Wesley and Russie, *Essential Works of John Wesley*, 1288.

they will know that it is not their job to do everything—some tasks are shared responsibilities. In the next chapter, church members are advised to take "The Criticism Commitment" by ensuring criticism is warranted, constructive, and kind.

7

The Criticism Commitment

*"One whose ear listens to a life-giving rebuke
will stay among the wise." —*PROVERBS 15:31

EDWARD MARKQUART RECORDS THE thoughts pastors often have after delivering a sermon: "'How did I do?' 'Was it okay?' 'Reassure me.'" He comments, "We ask these persistent questions because deep down inside, we're not sure we are okay. We need reassurance that we are loved and acceptable as preachers."[1]

No one likes to be criticized. The most common cause of harmful, unessential stress in pastors' lives is church members' tendency to engage in unconstructive criticism. While criticism extends to any vocation, circumstances could be more favorable for pastors to meet hostile criticism because of the public nature of their ministry, exposing them to further scrutiny. Many pastors are conscientious and hardworking, and so they often get discouraged when they don't meet their church members' expectations. When they come under criticism, they are tempted to redirect their attention and vigor away from their duty to study and preach God's word. Instead, they focus on the criticism, which is probably something of lesser consequence.

1. Markquart, *Quest for Better Preaching*, 63.

The Effects of Criticism and the Right to Criticize

Dave McClellan believes that it is "very normal to want to be a better preacher. It's very normal to want them to like you, even admire you."[2] He adds, "I don't think it's possible to purge our self-interest or self-awareness from preaching. It will always be present to some degree. It's impossible to stand up in front of people without a single concern over how we appear."[3] Tragically, this insecurity or self-doubt can puff up or crush pastors who mishandle feedback.

The feedback pastors often receive, as Jerry Vines and Jim L. Shaddix point out, is limited to two extremes: "overindulgent compliments or unforgiving criticisms. Consequently, most foyer feedback and email evaluations aren't objective and don't provide much useful material that can help a preacher progress and improve in his preaching."[4] Many pastors would be encouraged by just a little positive feedback from a few church members. As Luccock wrote, "Man cannot live by criticism alone."[5]

Criticism over any period can cause exasperation, insomnia, cynicism, burnout, and even despair.[6] Two research participants responded to the question, "When stressed, what makes you dread Sunday morning?" respectively: "Facing criticism for relatively unimportant issues (like toilets or light bulbs) when I should be focused on preaching." "I'll project all of my own criticisms onto the congregation and believe that they are all looking at me thinking the same things. As if they're all together asking, 'The church down the road had a packed parking lot, how come we don't?'"

Because of the doctrine of the priesthood of the believer, every believer may challenge a pastor. Pastors must remain able to welcome truthful inquiry, dissenting views, and even resistance to their leadership. As Spurgeon notes, "You must be able to bear

2. McClellan, *Preaching by Ear*, 7.

3. McClellan, *Preaching by Ear*, 17.

4. Vines and Shaddix, *Progress in the Pulpit*, 168.

5. Luccock, *In the Minister's Workshop*, 41.

6. Beeke and Thompson, *Pastors and Their Critics*, 16.

criticism, or you are not fit to be at the head of a congregation; and you must let the critic go without reckoning him among your deadly foes, or you will prove yourself a mere weakling."[7] Constructive criticism will keep pastors from false teaching and help them become more effective expositors. With all its surgical and invasive, but healing and restoring work, constructive criticism must have its place in the pastor's ministry.

The Criticism Commitment: Offer Feedback with Gentleness and Respect

Ensure criticism is warranted, constructive, and kind.

Pastors are not beyond criticism; they need it. However, feedback should be given to church leaders with gentleness and respect. "Obey your leaders and submit to them—for they keep watch over your souls as those who will give an account—so that they may do this with joy, not groaning; for this would be unhelpful for you" (Heb 13:17). Unconstructive criticism of a pastor leads to increased levels of stress. According to the results of the survey, the more a pastor is criticized, the more stressed they become. So it's important for both pastors and church members to learn how to give and receive constructive criticism in a healthy way. Pastors should be able to take criticism and use it to improve their ministry, while church members should be more understanding and supportive of their pastors.

Constructive vs. Unconstructive Criticism

Constructive criticism is expressed in accordance with biblical principles. It is a dissenting viewpoint expressed through due process, raising genuine questions aimed at problems rather than people, and is redemptive to all parties involved. "Constructive criticism

7. Spurgeon, *Lectures to My Students*, 326.

necessitates a measure of biblical optimism. If there is no hope of change, then there is nothing constructive about the criticism."[8]

Unconstructive criticism is opposed to biblical principles. It is generated outside due process, attacks a person rather than the problem, and is expressed in less than a redemptive spirit. Unconstructive criticism distresses pastors. It is stressful because it creates debilitating self-doubt and irrational guilt. The sympathetic pastor feels like any criticism would not be happening if he were doing his job better, and so it can cause unessential stress. The pastor may feel frustrated and lash out at others in anger.

When providing constructive feedback to your pastor, approach him with humility and understanding. Remove any ego from the equation, and only offer criticism if you believe it will be beneficial in helping him grow in his calling and not just making you feel better. Don't make any unfair judgment based on comparison to another minister or past experiences. Comparisons, in most cases, are not beneficial. Comparing your pastor to another pastor is an easy and unfair mistake to make. It overlooks individual circumstances. Every pastor is unique, with a different background and at different points in their ministerial journey. A simple, gentle reminder can be all that's needed for growth, and even then, they must know it comes from a place of love.

Measuring Success in Preaching

When it comes to preaching, how should pastors and church members measure success in preaching? The businessperson knows if their quotas have been met, the lawyer knows if their argument has won, and the student knows if they have passed. Oftentimes, a pastor's most effective sermons are rewarded with silence. The response is ambiguous.

Bryan Chapell reminds pastors that faithfulness to God and his word determines the success of a preacher. "When faithfulness to God becomes the primary aim of our preaching (and the

8. Beeke and Thompson, *Pastors and Their Critics*, 116.

grace of his love our greatest security), we are freed from inordinate concern about personal acceptance, reputation, and offense (Acts 4:29)."[9]

A sermon may always be improved, but God's word can never be improved. A pastor who has faithfully proclaimed God's word can rest in his preaching—the thunder shook Sinai, Elijah heard the still small voice, Jesus called his sheep, and Pentecost fire fell. The pastor should be content with such cosmic signs in the sky.

A Word to Pastors

Pastor, the sheep bite. In their book *Pastors and Their Critics*, Joel Beeke and Nicholas Thompson write that pastors must first come to terms with criticism being a part of the ministry. "Reckoning with this is an essential first step in dealing with it when it comes our way."[10] Receiving criticism is part of the job of a pastor. It is inevitable. There has never been a pastor who has not been the target of verbal opposition. Even Jesus, who was not deserving of criticism, was criticized.[11]

Pastors, Their Own Worst Critic

Many great preachers are critical of their own preaching. Augustine of Hippo, one of the greatest Christian preachers, said about his own preaching, "For my own way of expressing myself almost always disappoints me. I am anxious for the best possible, as I feel it in me before I start bringing it into the open in plain words: and when I see that it is less impressive than I had felt it to be, I am saddened that my tongue cannot live up to my heart."[12] Thomas Long, Patton Professor at Princeton Theological Seminary, responds to the question about what the hardest part of preaching is with this:

9. Chapell, *Christ-Centered Preaching*, 343.

10. Beeke and Thompson, *Pastors and Their Critics*, 52.

11. Beeke and Thompson, *Pastors and Their Critics*, 22.

12. Brown, *Augustine of Hippo*, 253.

"Writing from scratch and bringing an insight from the Bible is a grueling task." He then relates that this is the result of being harder on yourself than even your theology is.

There is a persistent feeling in preaching of wishing you could have been more effective. Pastors are so conscientious and reflective of their preaching because they must give an account for every word they say. Our words have eternal ramifications, and we don't feel like we measure up. We have doubts about our lack of preparation and prayer, as well as leading an upright, holy life to which we are calling our church members.

Add into the mix the personality types of many pastors. In his classic *Spiritual Depression*, Martyn Lloyd-Jones believes that introverts are more prone to spiritual depression than extroverts. An introverted person has heightened introspective tendencies, which can become a downward spiral into unhealthy levels of deep self-reflection and negativity. Lloyd-Jones diagnoses the prophet Jeremiah, John the Baptist, the apostle Paul, and the Reformer Luther with spiritual depression. That is a great company to belong to, but one must endure their particular vulnerabilities and subsequent trials.[13]

Contrary to the stereotype and traditional expectations of an outgoing, charismatic pastor being commonplace for many churches, research has revealed that the general personality profile of male clergy is low on the extraversion scale, which means most male clergy are introverts.[14] The demands of the pastor's social role are inherently challenging for an individual naturally predisposed towards a less extroverted personality type. This often results in feelings of stress, frustration, and failure. This dissonance leads some pastors to construct a public persona when it comes time to fulfill these social roles within their congregations, which results in an inaccurate representation of themselves.[15]

This does not mean introverts cannot succeed in the pastorate. The need for introverts in pastoral leadership roles should be

13. Lloyd-Jones, *Spiritual Depression*, 96.

14. Francis and Jones, *Psychological Perspectives on Christian Ministry*, 65.

15. Francis and Jones, *Psychological Perspectives on Christian Ministry*, 66.

embraced instead of questioned. Introverts may be more reflective than their extroverted counterparts, which means they may become better listeners and more sympathetic. They may have greater self-awareness, providing thoughtful leadership. Introversion is no barrier to pastoral success; it has its burdens and its advantages.

Pastors who are liable to intense introspection over their preaching must focus on the end they seek instead of their own self-approval. Markquart cites Brooks, who finds that focusing on the question "How shall I preach most effectively for others?" reduces the stress that comes from another question that preachers ask themselves: "How shall I do it most creditably for myself?" He urges, "The second question disappears out of your work just in proportion as the first question grows intense. . . . Care not for your servant, but for your truth and your people."[16] Markquart also refers to Lowell O. Erdahl, who maintains that "the best pulpit communication results from forgetting ourselves and remembering just two things: our truth and our people. . . . As the purpose of preaching is to call people out of self-centeredness into self-surrender and self-giving, so also the call of the Lord invites us to let go of ourselves and to preach with the abandonment of self-forgetfulness."[17]

Larsen reminds pastors that their eternal salvation does not depend on their good works or preaching performance. It is imperative that pastors embrace their acceptance in Christ and yield their spiritual poverty, self-confidence, and lack of attractiveness and gifting to him.[18] Pastor, give yourself some grace. Treat yourself just like how you would treat a member of your flock: be kind to yourself and don't put yourself down. You too must remember that you don't need to meet your own standards or the standards of others to be accepted and loved by God. Your and others' opinions do not dictate your intrinsic worth and value of being made in his image and redeemed by his blood.

16. Markquart, *Quest for Better Preaching*, 66.

17. Markquart, *Quest for Better Preaching*, 66.

18. Larsen, *Anatomy of Preaching*, 51.

How to Handle Criticism from Church Members

We've all been there before—a church member says something that hurts or makes us feel defensive, and our first instinct is to lash out. It's natural to want to protect ourselves, but as pastors, we are called to a higher standard. Navigating any criticism can be difficult and painful, especially when it is not rooted in genuine care or concern. We must use wisdom to discern malicious intent from those who too often take pleasure in bringing us down or seeing us hurt. It is easy to let our emotions cloud our judgment and fall victim to the opinion of someone who just wants us to stumble. Scripture tells us, again and again, to turn the other cheek, love our enemies, and forgive those who sin against us. So how do we do that? How do we take criticism without getting defensive?

REMEMBER, CRITICISM IS AN INVITATION TO TRUST IN GOD.

Beeke and Thompson teach that the Lord uses verbal critique to humble his preachers. He wields criticism to expose their blind spots.[19] Frank B. Minirth and Paul D. Meier argue that handling criticism, "dealing responsibly with the truth about ourselves through the power of God and the insights of close friends," is part of Christian sanctification.[20] So, see criticism for what it is: an invitation to trust in God, grow closer to him, and become more like him. It's not easy, but it's worth it. One of the best things about receiving criticism is that it forces us to take a good, hard look at ourselves. Pastor, just like we cannot rely on others' opinions about us for our approval, we can also never rely on our own opinion about ourselves for our approval. Often, we are too close to a situation to see ourselves, but when someone else points out our flaws, it allows us to see things differently and make changes accordingly. This process of introspection can be hard, but it is essential for our spiritual maturity.

19. Beeke and Thompson, *Pastors and Their Critics*, 98–99.
20. Minirth and Meier, *Happiness Is a Choice*, 60.

When you receive criticism, also consider it as an opportunity to humble yourself before God and learn more about his will for your ministry. It is a blessing to be humble. It's easy to get cocky when things are going well, but when someone criticizes us, it brings us back down to earth and reminds us that we are not perfect. This humility is essential for believers because it allows us to see ourselves the way God sees us—as fallen sinners in need of his grace and mercy. Also, as pastors, we are tasked with leading our congregations and helping others grow in their faith. We cannot do this effectively if we are not open to honest feedback and willing to listen when others criticize us. Only through humility and a willingness to learn will we be able to truly serve our flock and fulfill God's will for our lives and ministries.

PRAY AND ASK GOD TO HELP YOU HANDLE CRITICISM.

Begg and Prime offer insight for when a church member complains and the pastor cannot discuss it immediately. While the pastor should insist on setting an appointment to address the issue later, he should pray with that individual right then and there. Say, "We will discuss this more later, but let's pray for God's assistance now." This has multiple benefits. It demonstrates that the concern is the Lord's. It softens the attitude of the critic, and it emphasizes church unity. No church member could refuse such wisdom and blessing. Anything worth discussing is worthy of prayer.[21]

Massey confesses, "Without the Spirit's assistance, the pressures of inwardness and anxiety can spell death unless a preacher relies prayerfully on God."[22] Clergy who pray frequently have better vitality, as well as general and mental health scores.[23] The pressures of ministry are great, and the temptation to give up is strong. Yet, we must never lose sight of the fact that our hope and strength

21. Prime and Begg, *On Being a Pastor*, 77–78.
22. Massey, *Burdensome Joy of Preaching*, 20.
23. Meisenhelder and Chandler, "Frequency of Prayer," 323.

come from God alone. One of the most important ways that we can stay connected to God is through prayer.

Prayer is essential for pastors for many reasons. First, prayer reminds us that we are not alone. In our isolation, we are tempted to believe that God is there for others, but not for us. This is a lie from the enemy designed to keep us from experiencing the fullness of God's love. But when we pray, we are reminded that we are not alone in this world, even in our darkest hours.

Second, prayer is not just about getting things from God; it is also about giving things to him. Prayer provides us with the opportunity to share our concerns and burdens with him. It is a time for us to lay everything before him and to let go of our worries and fears. When we do so, it shows that we trust him enough to deal with our deepest concerns. It also demonstrates our commitment to following his will for our lives. We surrender our plans and dreams to his perfect will and ask that he would use us for his glory.

Third, prayer gives us the strength to handle criticism. When we rely on God in prayer, we are tapping into a source of strength that is greater than ourselves. We are acknowledging our dependence on him and his power to work in our lives. In prayer, we can find the peace and strength that we need to handle criticism.

READ THE SCRIPTURES TO GAIN WISDOM ON CRITICISM.

The Bible has a lot to say that applies to giving and receiving criticism. For example, as Christians, we are called to love our neighbor as ourselves (Matt 22:39). This includes being mindful of how we speak to others and receive criticism. Proverbs 12:1–5 teaches us about the importance of loving knowledge and discipline. It also says that the thoughts of the righteous are just and the counsels of the wicked are deceitful. This is a good reminder not to hate reproof but to be seekers of the truth. It also admonishes us to be suspicious of and avoid the counsel of wicked, deceitful people.

In Matt 7:1–5, Jesus commands us not to judge others wrongly because the same standards that we use he will use on us. He says we should look at our own faults before critiquing others.

This teaches us the importance of being self-aware and taking our own egos out of the equation when giving feedback. Romans 12:17–21 says to repay no one evil for evil, to give thought to do what is honorable in everyone's eyes, to live at peace with everyone as far as possible, and to persevere in tribulation. This is instructive on how we can respond respectfully to people who have unkind opinions about us.

COLLABORATE WITH TRUSTED LAY LEADERS ABOUT CRITICISM.

Some criticism is warranted and can be helpful in making you a better pastor; other times, it can be overwhelming and make you feel like the world is against you. So how do you know when to listen to criticism and when to tune it out? Just because someone is critical of you doesn't mean that everyone is. And on the flip side, just because someone praises you doesn't mean that you're doing everything right. So, pastor, don't overgeneralize criticism or praise. One vocal person rarely speaks for many or God.

Another critical thing to keep in mind is that not all criticism is created equal. One research participant, in response to the question "What is the most important thing you do to prevent experiencing high levels of exhaustion and stress?" answered, "Every criticism is not worth the same amount of time. Sort them and then decide if it's worth your time and energy." In *This Odd and Wondrous Calling*, Martin B. Copenhaver notes, "I let myself value the opinion of some people more than others. One way to sort this out is to ask myself, 'Would I seek out this person's opinion?' If not, then why would I give it much weight?" One minister spoke regrettably, "It was only when it was too late that I realized that I had spent all that time listening to the wrong people."[24] Is the person who gave the criticism someone whose opinion you value? Would you go to that person and ask him for his view on another important subject? If you don't value their opinion about other matters, why does

24. Daniel and Copenhaver, *This Odd and Wondrous Calling*, loc. 2013–14.

their opinion of you matter now? That's why it's helpful to seek the counsel of a trusted lay leader when you're feeling overwhelmed by criticism. They likely have a perspective that you don't, and they can help you see the situation more clearly.

Pastors are oftentimes lone wolves. They find themselves without close friends or feel isolated from their congregation. Just because pastors are used to giving support doesn't mean they don't need it. Pastors are more likely to feel lonely than those in non-pastoral roles.[25] That's why it's so important for pastors to have social support—a group of people in their lives whom they can rely on for care, love, and appreciation both personally and professionally.[26] Yet clergy often report feeling they do not have the proper support from church members or church leadership to perform their assigned duties.

Furthermore, pastors often avoid discussing their personal lives with church members for fear of being perceived as weak. Intrapersonal styles of coping—strategies that don't involve interactions with others—are the most commonly used self-care strategies among clergy.[27] This furthers the idea that pastors may not be prioritizing personal social interactions and relationships. How can pastors seek the counsel of a trusted lay leader to discern whether or not a criticism is valid when they don't even have close friends in the church?

Pastors and lay leaders should answer at least one question to weigh criticism carefully. Theologian Lauren Winner mentions a technique used by art critic Peter Schjeldahl when he despises a piece. "He questions himself, 'What would I like about this if I liked it?'" Pastors and lay leaders may ask this about the most callous critique.[28] It's easy to get wrapped up in the negativity of criticism and forget that there might be some truth to what the person is saying. If you can't see the kernel of truth in what

25. Warner and Carter, "Loneliness, Marital Adjustment and Burnout," 125.

26. Carr et at., "As Social Support," 385.

27. McMinn et al., "Care for Pastors," 563.

28. Proeschold-Bell and Byassee, *Faithful and Fractured*, 51.

they're saying, then ask yourself why are you giving the criticism so much weight. Pastor, don't regret spending your time listening to all the wrong people.

ENGAGE IN PHYSICAL ACTIVITY TO RELIEVE THE STRESS OF CRITICISM.

One way to help relieve some of the stress that comes with criticism is by engaging in some physical activity. Sure, you might not have time for a long run or a trip to the gym every day, but there are plenty of other ways to get your heart rate up and reduce stress. Taking a brisk walk outside or even doing some simple stretching at home can make a world of difference. Not only will you feel better physically, but you'll also notice an improvement in your mental and emotional state as well. When you engage in physical activity, your body releases endorphins. These "feel-good" chemicals have mood-boosting effects that can help you feel calmer and more positive. Physical activity also provides a sense of accomplishment. When people feel like they are doing something worthwhile, it can boost their confidence. So next time you're feeling overwhelmed by criticism, take some time to move your body.

RESPOND TO CRITICISM WITH GRACE.

It's easy to feel defensive when we are criticized. We may want to argue or justify our actions, but it is important to respond with grace. By staying calm and polite, we can show that we are willing to listen and learn. In addition, by responding with grace, we can also show the other person that we're willing to try to see their point of view and work together towards a resolution. True strength isn't found in getting the last word but being able to take criticism without getting defensive and instead trying to understand where the other person is coming from.

When we are feeling hurt and angry after being criticized, it can be tempting to hold on to those feelings and nurse our grievances. But Christ calls us to forgive those who sin against us (Luke 6:37). Forgiveness is essential for our physical and mental health. Still, more importantly, forgiveness is necessary for our spiritual health because it allows us to experience the fullness of God's love and grace. When we respond to criticism with grace, we are modeling Christ-like behavior. We are showing that we are willing to forgive and move on. This does not mean that the hurt does not sting or that what happened was okay. It simply means that we are choosing to react in a way that is honoring to God.

Summary

Church members are called to listen to their pastors, but whom should pastors listen to? There are many voices, and it can be difficult to discern which ones are worth listening to. It's easy to get caught up in the noise and end up taking advice that leads us astray. First and foremost, pastors should listen to the voice of God in his word, which is our foundation for life and ministry. It is his will that we seek above all else. Other voices should take a back seat to his. But what about other voices? Are there any that we should lend an ear to? Yes, there are. We should listen to those who love us and who will tell us the truth, even when it's hard to hear. They will challenge us and push us to be better. They will hold us accountable and help us stay on track.

As pastors, we will face criticism. It comes with the territory. Criticism can be brutal, but it's crucial that we remember our role as leaders and respond accordingly. When we take the high road and respond with grace, we show our congregation that we are capable of humility and forgiveness. These are essential qualities for any effective leader, and they are qualities that will help us build strong relationships within our congregation. The next time you are faced with criticism, take a moment to breathe and pray. Ask God for the grace to respond in a way that will honor him. Remember, how you react speaks volumes about your faith. Choose to respond with grace. In the next chapter, church members are called to take up "The Remembrance Commitment," to encourage their pastors to remember their call to ministry.

8

The Remembrance Commitment

*"The pulpit calls those anointed to it as the sea calls its sailors;
and like the sea, it batters and bruises, and does not rest. . . .
To preach, to really preach, is to die naked a little at a time
and to know each time you do it that you must do it again."*
—Bruce Thieleman[1]

MY PARENTS ENROLLED ME in Cramerton Christian Academy in seventh grade. The principal, Mr. Brown, and faculty would go far beyond just positively complementing the instruction I was receiving from my home and church. They played an integral role in my spiritual formation. On my first day, my homeroom teacher, Jason Barnhill, kindly nagged me because I was the only kid not from the Cramerton area. I was soon given the nickname "Lincolnton" after my hometown.

Oddly enough, a couple of weeks later, that joke would be a turning point in my life. The nominations for class chaplain were called. The class chaplain was responsible for sharing a ten-minute devotion from the Bible with the class every morning before the school day began. My new friend Matt Robinson shouted, "What about ol' Lincolnton!" Before I knew what was happening, my peers had elected me to the role. This little experience would have a seismic influence on my life. What began as an act of levity was

1. Johnson, "To Preach, to Really Preach."

soon met with unexpected gravity. The responsibility shaped me and made me take God's word seriously.

In my eighth-grade year, I had a transforming experience. Cramerton Christian Academy took a week-long spiritual retreat to a camp named The Wilds. For years, since a Vacation Bible School at my home church, I struggled with the gap between repentance and trusting Jesus as my righteousness. I tried to make myself worthy by disciplining myself to be a good Christian. After hearing a powerful, sobering sermon on the reality of hell during an evening service at camp, this mentality was deeply challenged. Trying was not enough; my only hope is Christ alone. His death and resurrection are my righteousness. That night, God's mercy broke down all the barriers so true salvation could take hold in my heart! In humble acknowledgment of this truth, I was overcome with emotion, but, with tears streaming down my cheeks in plain view, I was too embarrassed to seek counsel immediately.

After the auditorium emptied, my good friend Adam Eberhart asked me to go along with him in approaching Bro. Eric Simpson, our school's student minister, to pray for an issue. I agreed, hoping I would have a chance to talk to Bro. Eric myself. After we prayed, I broke down, laying my heart open before Bro. Eric and Adam. At that moment, beneath the weight of sin, Bro. Eric, with calm wisdom and understanding, reminded me of Rom 10:9: "that if you confess with your mouth Jesus as Lord, and believe in your heart that God raised Him from the dead, you will be saved." For the first time, I was able to "get it." It finally "clicked." I cried out to Jesus, and peace with God flooded my heart and mind.

God granted me more opportunities to share his word with more of those around me—from my fellow classmates to students across grade levels during my tenth through twelfth-grade years when I served as student body chaplain. My passion for teaching God's word persuaded many mature believers to believe God was calling me into full-time Christian ministry. Ann Chambers and other precious elderly ladies from my home church told me they prayed regularly for me to recognize my calling, but I was immature and would have none of it. Bro. Eric often called me a "preacher boy," which I took offense to because I wanted nothing to do with outright surrendering to full-time Christian ministry.

Honestly, I wanted the best of both worlds. I wanted to live for myself and serve in the local church without accepting responsibility for leading or overseeing it! I became so self-centered that when I was given opportunities to teach in church and school, I made it a point that I was not "preaching" but simply "speaking." Clearly, I was preaching. Outwardly I would claim that my messages were not sermons, but I would admit to myself now and then how much enjoyment I received from proclaiming God's word.

In eleventh grade, my school asked me to represent them in the sermonette category of an event hosted by the Southern Association of Christian Schools. SACS would assemble to display their talents, be critiqued, and be awarded. I welcomed the opportunity. After delivering my devotion that day, I remember being overwhelmed with joy. For the first time, I optimistically considered the call to ministry. Then something inside me shifted: here lay his call upon me all along, but I refused to heed it.

That night in my hotel, kneeling at the threshold between what had been and where God was taking me, I surrendered my life to the ministry. I prayed that God would make me the man he wanted me to be. The next opportunity I was given to preach at my church, I announced my acceptance of the call to full-time Christian ministry. Following the service, I went and apologized and thanked those elderly ladies whom I had looked down on for affirming God's call on my life.

Downplaying the Call

Kent and Barbara Hughes note that it is popular today to downplay the call to ministry. Some ministers believe that their job is just like any other profession, like being a lawyer or banker. Additionally, some people argue that we should downplay the call to ministry in order to close the gap between pastors and church members. They argue that professionals should see their jobs as a ministry. However, what they fail to realize is that while God calls people to various lives, the ministry is distinctive because it is a calling to nourish souls.[2]

Defining the Call

According to the *Concise Encyclopedia of Preaching*, the call to preach is a summons from God to proclaim the gospel. It is compelling and urgent. "The preacher must speak because God has provided a message. There is no other choice." As Martin Luther King, Sr. said of his son, "The boy was called to preach. He had to be; he could do no other."[3] Hans van der Geest conveys the call to preach as a personal engagement by God to preach his word to others. "A preacher would be crippled without a consciousness of being called."[4]

In *The New Guidebook for Pastors*, Mac Brunson and James Bryant write that there is no substitute for the call to ministry. "If you are in the ministry and do not have a clear, unquestionable sense of God's call, even though you may not be able to explain it, then you should leave the ministry immediately. The harm you can do to people, a congregation, your family, yourself, and the kingdom is beyond description." Brunson and Bryant continue, "There will be many times when the only thing that holds your hand to the plow is your call."[5]

Matt Bloom of the University of Notre Dame interviewed pastors and invited them to share the story of their call to ministry. Then, in follow-up interviews, he asked them to recount the story of their call to ministry once more. Bloom discovered that while everything is going well in their church, a pastor's recollection of his call to ministry is clearer and more certain. However, when their church is undergoing difficult times, the pastor's

---

2. Hughes and Hughes, *Liberating Ministry*, loc. 1422.

3. Lischer and William, *Concise Encyclopedia of Preaching*, 59.

4. Lischer, *Theories of Preaching*, 82.

5. Brunson and Bryant, *New Guidebook for Pastors*, 32.

memory of his call to ministry is hazy.[6] Pastors should recollect their call to ministry and write it down so they can revisit it on these stressful days.

Despising the Call

While the call to ministry may make pastors want to do their job well, it can also cause them to work longer hours. As calling intensity increases, work hours increase. People with intense callings have a harder time psychologically detaching from work, which can mean they don't get enough sleep and aren't as energetic in the morning.[7] Ken Pargament and Annette Mahoney have developed the concept of Sanctification Theory. It says that when people give sacred meaning to something, they work hard for it, protect it, and get upset if it is taken away. Because their work is sacred, clergy might consider everything they do as equally important. This can lead to them working too much and not taking care themselves very well.[8] Pastors may also feel that the stakes are higher. They may feel that they have more to lose if they fail, and more to gain if they are successful.[9] This also means they may be more sensitive to criticism from church members.[10]

Spurgeon illustrates how having an intense calling subjects ministers to melancholy. When pastors undertake this task seriously, they become susceptible to depression. Shouldering souls will lead the pastor to feel like he is sinking to the ground. His soul becomes overwhelmed with anxiety and disappointment when he sees how much work is not fulfilled, as if it ever will. It is more than enough to make pastors lose hope when they watch saints fail, do unbecoming things, and advance in their wickedness. Their desires and expectations have not been met, and so

---

6. Proeschold-Bell and Byassee, *Faithful and Fractured*, 22–23.

7. Clinton et al., "It's Tough Hanging-Up a Call," 28.

8. Pargament and Mahoney, "Sacred Matters."

9. Meek et al., "Maintaining Personal Resiliency," 345.

10. Proeschold-Bell et al., "Using Effort-Reward Imbalance Theory," 439.

pastors must grieve. When people still disbelieve the preacher's report, how can the preacher not be sad?[11]

On the other hand, Massey, quoting Gardner Taylor, still believes that it is the call to preach that instills pastors with boldness to face the stresses of preaching: "It is in the strength of a divinely-given call to preach that the preacher will rightly deal with the concern for 'enough inner security.'"[12] So which is it: is having a strong sense of calling to ministry a liability or an asset?

The Remembrance Commitment: Remember His Ministry

Recognize his call at ministerial anniversaries
as a sign of appreciation.

When pastors answered how they identify themselves to others, their stress levels go up or down depending on how strongly they agree or disagree with the following statement: "The first thing I often think about when I describe myself to others is that I'm a preacher." This means that for pastors who identify more as preachers, preaching causes less stress. While pastors who identify less as preachers, preaching causes more stress.

So, is having a strong sense of calling to ministry a liability or asset? According to this research, Gardner Taylor was correct. It is an asset. Even though Spurgeon forewarned of the call to ministry's dark side, he would also concur that "if any brother here is not assured of his call to the ministry, let him wait till he is sure of it."[13] Many research participants noticed the coping effect of calling intensity. When asked, "How would you advise pastors to prepare themselves for preaching stress?" one research participant succinctly stated, "1) Know you are called; 2) Pray; 3) Do the hard work of preparation; 4) Present your sermon as an act of worship

11. Spurgeon, *Lectures to My Students*, 156.

12. Massey, *Burdensome Joy of Preaching*, 25.

13. Spurgeon, *All-Round Ministry*, 20–21.

to the Lord; 5) Be honest with the text and its presentation to the congregation." Pastors do not attempt the impossible on their own. They have been called and sent by God, and that is sufficient.

One of the best ways church members can help their pastors is by taking the time to recognize their call on ministerial anniversaries. Pastors who serve well deserve honor and appreciation, and a ministerial anniversary is a perfect time to remind your pastor why they chose this path and to thank them for everything they've done. As you approach ministerial anniversaries, take a moment in your service to honor your pastor and ask them to relay to the congregation their call to ministry. Recognizing his call is a simple but effective way for you to take care of your pastor and remind him why he decided to dedicate his life to this calling in the first place.

There is one more way church members can ensure their pastors have the time and support they need to focus on their well-being. To be effective in their ministries, pastors must take time to care for themselves physically and mentally. Unfortunately, many pastors typically say yes to others before themselves, and if they say no, they feel guilty about taking the time. As a result, their own well-being often takes a backseat to the demands of the ministry. It is crucial for churches to proactively give permission for pastors to focus on their own health. On a ministerial anniversary, make it clear to the rest of the congregation that your church supports your pastor in taking care of himself to help reduce stress and burnout. By publicly, privately, and repeatedly giving pastors permission to spend time on themselves, church members can ensure that their health and well-being are always a priority. This may seem small, but it will free your pastor to focus on their health.[14]

A Word to Pastors

There will be dark times in the ministry. There will be moments when you question why you even entered the ministry and if

14. Proeschold-Bell and Byassee, *Faithful and Fractured*, 24.

you have just been a failure. In those dark nights of the soul, it is essential to remember what ministry success looks like. Unlike mowing the grass, preaching does not produce a tangible "product" after a sermon. No single number, not even attendance, could label a pastor as "productive." Getting caught up in thinking of success in terms of numbers is easy. How many people showed up to church this week? But when it comes to preaching, numbers can be deceiving. In the parable of the sower (Matt 13:1–23), Jesus teaches us that initial responses to the gospel message could prove misleading over time.[15]

You might think, "But surely there must be some metric by which we can measure success in ministry." And you're right, there is. But it's not attendance, offering totals, or any other external measure. So how can we measure whether or not a pastor is successful? The answer is found in faithfulness. The only way to gauge whether a pastor is successful is by their faithfulness to Scripture. Are they teaching God's word accurately? Are they living in obedience to what they preach? Those are the only things that matter. A successful pastor is, first and foremost, faithful to God's word. They study diligently and pray earnestly, seeking to build their sermons on the foundation of Scripture. They are also faithful in their personal lives, striving to live holy lives that reflect the truth of the Scripture they preach. In an age where pastors increasingly fall prey to moral failures, faithfulness is more important than ever. So the key to being a successful pastor is not to generate a large following or be popular for a time. Instead, a successful pastor is faithful to teaching and living by the word.

Faithfulness is difficult, especially when we do not see any good happening. However, we need to remember what Spurgeon noted: "Success belongs to God; service belongs to us."[16] Our obedience is to God, not to the results of our efforts. We live in a consumer culture that seeks immediate gratification, but unfortunately, the ministry doesn't work like that. Growth takes time, and there will always be ups and downs. The key is to maintain your focus and

15. "What Is Success in Ministry?"
16. Spurgeon, "Sure Triumph."

keep plowing ahead even when you feel like you're getting nowhere. The fact of the matter is that we don't know when or how God will bless our efforts. We just need to be faithful and trust that he will do what is best. Remember, our goal is not success but faithfulness; not attendance but obedience; not speed but perseverance. Endure! Don't give up on your ministry! Keep proclaiming the good news of Jesus Christ until he comes!

Pastor, beware of social media. It's no secret that social media can be a source of jealousy and comparison. This is equally true for pastors, who are often pressured to project a particular image. This puts tremendous pressure on the pastor to maintain a confident persona in real life and online. Not only do they have to be the church's spiritual leaders, but they also have to be dynamic, engaging, and relatable. It's no wonder 80 percent of pastors feel envious of other pastors' success.[17]

Sally Morgenthaler writes, "Pastors know how to edit their lives for public consumption."[18] The trouble with social media is that it gives us a false sense of reality. It's easy to look at other pastors' perfectly curated feeds and think they have it all together. We then compare our behind-the-scenes to their highlight reels. But every pastor has an ugly side that often isn't captured in a photo or status update. Do you find yourself feeling down after mindlessly scrolling through your feed? Do you compare your life to the highlights reel of other pastors and feel like you aren't keeping up?

If you're struggling with social media envy, take a break. Pick up a book, go for a walk, or talk to a friend instead. Be mindful of how much time you're spending on social media. It can be helpful to set some boundaries around your use of social media. For example, you could decide to only check social media at certain times of the day or use it for specific purposes such as connecting with friends and family. Finally, remember that social media is just a snapshot of our lives. It doesn't give the whole picture. We are more than the sum of our Instagram pictures and Facebook posts.

17. Briggs, "Why Are Pastors Depressed?"

18. Morgenthaler, "Does Ministry Fuel Addictive Behavior?"

We must remember why we preach in the first place. It's not because of us; it's because he called. It has always and only been a matter of him. We preach not because we are good but because he is good and he cares for his people. So if we preach, it must be because we care first and foremost about him. So let us preach with humility, knowing that it is God who calls, saves, and changes lives. Let us preach with boldness, knowing that the gospel is the power of God unto salvation (Rom 1:16). And let us preach with joy, knowing that as we proclaim Christ crucified and resurrected, his glory shines forth for all the world to see (2 Cor 4:5–6).

Summary

Churches should not downplay the call to preach, and pastors should not enter ministry lightly. They have a deep calling from God to serve his people in this way. Once they answer the call, they must stick with it even when it's tough. They must not give up when they don't see results right away or when they experience difficult seasons. Being faithfully committed like this requires immense courage and strength—two things that can only come from God himself.

We see that the true measure of a successful pastor is not numbers or popularity but faithfulness. When we view success through this lens, we realize that even the most popular preacher may not be successful in God's eyes if they are not faithful. And conversely, even the most obscure pastor may be highly successful in God's sight if they are faithfully committed to his word. So let us all strive for faithfulness in our preaching and personal lives! In the next chapter, there is a final word to churches, local associations, state conventions, seminaries, homileticians, and pastors.

9

Conclusion: Sisyphus

"Ours is not the unrequited toil of Sisyphus . . ." —Charles Spurgeon[1]

It's no secret that the role of a pastor is a demanding one. There are many factors that contribute to the stress that pastors feel. The research found that—with the proliferation of pastoral duties, the disparity in congregational priorities, unrealistic expectations, and few uninterrupted blocks of time for study—preaching and sermon preparation can be quite stressful. Another key influence on pastoral stress is criticism. Many pastors feel like they can never please everyone and that they are constantly under scrutiny.

This stress can have negative effects on a pastor's health, relationships, and ability to do their job. When a pastor is stressed, they may find it difficult to sleep, eat properly, or exercise regularly. This can lead to physical problems such as obesity, high blood pressure, and heart disease. Pastoral stress can also lead to mental health problems such as anxiety, depression, and burnout. In addition, pastoral stress can damage relationships with family members, friends, and church members. Stress can also make it difficult for a pastor to focus on their sermon and prepare adequately for worship services. There are some things that church members and pastors can do to help reduce the stress pastors feel, especially as it relates to sermon preparation and preaching.

1. Spurgeon, *All-Round Ministry*, 24.

The Seven Commitments of a Preach Well Church

A supportive congregation—one that understands and values the role of the pastor—can almost single-handedly address the majority of pastoral stress. When church members make an effort to understand and empathize with their pastor's challenges instead of adding to them, it can go a long way toward reducing stress. In contrast, an unsupportive congregation can be one of the biggest sources of stress for a pastor. Common complaints from pastors include criticism from church members and congregations who make demands on the pastor's time that are unreasonable. Just knowing that they have the support of their congregation can make all the difference for pastors who are struggling with burnout. Pastors are human beings too, and they need the church's support just as much as the church needs theirs. A supportive congregation provides an environment where the pastor can preach well. This support takes the form of the seven commitments of a Preach Well Church.

1. **The Control Commitment: Relinquish Control of Your Pastor's Schedule**

   Acknowledge that, due to the nature of ministry, the pastor's work cannot be rigidly regulated.

2. **The Expectations Commitment: Review Expectations and Priorities for Mutuality**

   Annually ensure that the agreed-upon expectations and priorities of the pastor are observed and adjusted when required, permitting him to discuss potential problems.

3. **The Appointment Commitment: Make an Appointment**

   Defend the pastor's sermon preparation time from all unnecessary interruptions.

4. **The Honor Commitment: Honor the Word by Providing for Your Pastor and Prioritizing his Wellness**

   Annually review the pastor's financial agreements and time arrangements and insist that he takes weekly time off and annual vacations to spend on his personal needs and with his family.

5. **The Volunteer Commitment: Embrace Church Members Discipling and Visiting**

   Affirm the pastor's biblical freedom to delegate ministry to capable church members.

6. **The Criticism Commitment: Offer Feedback with Gentleness and Respect**

   Ensure criticism is warranted, constructive, and kind.

7. **The Remembrance Commitment: Remember His Ministry**

   Recognize his call at ministerial anniversaries as a sign of appreciation.

Beyond these, pray for him. This one might seem like a no-brainer, but it's worth repeating: pastors need our prayers! Pastors need all the prayers they can get! They need your spiritual support first and foremost. So take some time out each day to lift up your pastor in prayer. Ask God to give them wisdom, courage, and strength as they lead the flock entrusted to them. Ask your pastor if there is any particular request that he would like you to pray for him on a regular basis.

In *Only a Prayer Meeting*, Spurgeon mentions receiving a prayer request from a minister who often asked Spurgeon and his church to pray for his severe depression that kept him from pursuing his pastoral duties. Spurgeon encourages us to pray for the healing of such pastors.[2] This is something that we can all do. When we see a struggling pastor, let us remember to lift them up in prayer. We can always be their prayer support. Let us not

---

2. Spurgeon, *Only a Prayer Meeting*, 32–33.

forget those who are fighting their battles while trying to lead others in theirs.

Encourage your pastor on a regular basis. If you've been particularly blessed by a sermon, take the time to let your pastor know. A simple handwritten note or brief email expressing your gratitude can go a long way. You could even make a point to speak with them after services on Sundays and let them know how much you enjoyed the sermon and what points really spoke to you personally. Be specific. In today's society, it seems like there's always someone who is quick to criticize but slow to offer words of encouragement. Don't be one of those people! Make it a habit to encourage your pastor on a regular basis, both privately and publicly.

Offer to help them in any way you can. We all know that time is one commodity that pastors often don't have enough of! So if you have specific talents or skills that might be of use to your pastor or your church, offer to help out in any way you can! Whether it's helping with administrative tasks or volunteer opportunities, or just offering up a listening ear, visiting, paying for a sitter so they can have some free time, or helping out at the church, anything you can do to lighten your pastor's load is always appreciated.

Remember, supporting your pastor doesn't have to be complicated or expensive. When you take the time to show your support, you are not only making their job easier but also making your church stronger (Heb 13:5). It's clear that having a supportive congregation is vital to a pastor's well-being and his preaching effectiveness. When church members work together with their pastor as allies instead of adversaries, it makes for a much healthier and less stressful church community overall.

How Local Associations and State Conventions Can Help

Local associations and state conventions impact thousands of pastors across America. They play an important role in supporting pastors. Here are five suggestions that local associations and state conventions can consider to help mitigate pastoral stress.

1. Launch a Campaign

One of the best ways to help pastors deal with stress is to increase awareness of the issue among church members, especially how criticism and congregational support affects pastors. Campaigns may include sermon, small group, and educational materials. With a heightened awareness of pastoral stress, congregations can be more understanding and supportive of their pastor. Also, normalizing the difficulties that pastors face lets pastors know they are not alone. Be sure to leverage social media to engage local church members directly. Pastors may be hesitant to bring up these subjects in their churches. Social media provides a direct line of communication between local and state leaders and the congregation.

2. Encourage Spouses

The spouse of a pastor bears a unique burden. They are often their best friend and biggest supporter. As such, they play a vital role in mitigating pastoral stress. It's crucial for state conventions and local associations to encourage pastor's spouses by affirming their role in ministry and offering support specifically for spouses of pastors. This could take the form of seminars, counseling services, or even just regular social get-togethers where spouses can connect with one another.

3. Promote Self-Care

Another way that associations and conventions can help pastors deal with pastoral stress is by promoting self-care. This means encouraging pastors to take care of their physical, emotional, and mental health. Additionally, it may also involve providing resources like counseling, retreats for pastors and their spouses, burnout prevention tips, and even financial assistance for self-care expenses.

4. Train Lay Leaders

When lay leaders are adequately trained, they are better equipped to handle many of the responsibilities that would otherwise fall on the shoulders of the pastor—such as leading Bible studies or effectively leading worship services in the absence of the pastor. By taking some of these responsibilities off the pastor's plate, lay leaders can help reduce pastoral stress.

5. Fill Pulpits on Short Notice

Finally, state conventions and local associations can help reduce pastoral stress by filling pulpits on short notice when pastors are unable to preach due to illness or emergency. Not having pulpit supply can add even more stress to an already difficult situation. By having a pool of qualified lay people who are willing and able to step in at a moment's notice, state conventions and local associations can help take some of the pressure off their pastors.

The Role of Seminaries and Homileticians

Seminaries need to equip their students with the tools they need to handle the stress of the pastorate. One way to do this is in pastoral method courses, by addressing subjects like how to take congregational criticism and what some coping resources to mitigate pastoral stress are. Seminaries should also assign a paper to first-year pastors to recollect and write out their call to ministry. After submission, it should be discussed and then returned so they can keep it.

Additionally, seminaries should not shy away from critiquing their students. As John Broadus, the father of modern expository preaching, noted, "One of the chief sources of instruction in homiletics is the criticism of instructors or judicious hearers upon our own preaching."[3] One of the most valuable aspects of a seminary education is receiving criticism from professors in preaching class. Seminary is a prime time for students to embrace constructive criticism.[4] By receiving specific and meaningful feedback, pastors-in-training can learn how to handle congregational criticism.

A Final Word to Pastors

You Are Not Alone!

If you are a pastor reading this, remember you are not alone in feeling stressed about your role. In 2 Tim 4:9–10, Paul says to Timothy, "Make every effort to come to me soon; for Demas, having loved this present world, has deserted me and gone to Thessalonica; Crescens has gone to Galatia, Titus to Dalmatia. Only Luke is with me." We see that even Paul didn't always have the support he needed. People deserted him, and it made ministry difficult. Still, he kept pressing on because he knew he wasn't alone in ministry. "At my first defense no one supported me, but all deserted me; may it not be counted against them. But the Lord stood with me and strengthened me, so that through me the proclamation might be fully accomplished, and that all the Gentiles might hear; and I was rescued out of the lion's mouth" (2 Tim 4:16–18). We serve a God who doesn't leave us alone to fend for ourselves. Jesus promised never to leave or forsake us. So when things are tough and it feels like we can't go on, we need to remember that we are not alone in ministry. We serve a faithful God who will never abandon us.

It Is Rewarding!

Despite the challenges of being a pastor, it is still rewarding. As a pastor, you get to help people through tough times—such as

3. Broadus, *On the Preparation*, 37.

4. Beeke and Thompson, *Pastors and Their Critics*, 152–53

illness, divorce, or the death of a loved one—and rejoice with them during the good times—such as births, baptisms, and weddings. Even though being a pastor is difficult, it is still worth it because we know that our reward awaits us in heaven. Remember that there is reserved for you an unfading crown of glory (2 Tim 4:8). So let us not grow weary in well-doing but let us persevere knowing that God will reward us generously.

Take Care of Yourself!

One of young pastor Timothy's pastoral responsibilities was to keep a close watch on himself. "Pay close attention to yourself and to the teaching; persevere in these things, for as you do this you will save both yourself and those who hear you" (1 Tim 4:16). Self-care is foundational to congregational care.[5] Self-care is not selfish; it is essential. We cannot give what we do not have. In order to effectively care for others, we must first take care of ourselves. This means that we must make time for rest and relaxation, exercise and healthy eating, and spiritual disciplines such as prayer and Bible study. When we neglect our own needs, we are not able to effectively meet the needs of others.

E. M. Bounds notes that preaching is not a one-hour performance. "It is the outflow of a life. It takes twenty years to make a sermon, because it takes twenty years to make the man."[6] The preaching develops as the pastor develops. The sermon is persuasive because the pastor is persuasive. The preaching is strong because the pastor is strong. The pastor's life affects how a sermon is developed and delivered. Preaching is a lifestyle. If preaching is to have only one primary concern, it should be no one element of preaching itself but the pastor himself.

The pastor himself matters to God. Methodist preacher William Quayle asked this: Is preaching the practice of developing and presenting a sermon? No, that is not preaching. "Preaching

5. Belleville, *Commentary on 1 Timothy*, 88.

6. Bounds, *Essential Works*, loc. 109

is the art of making a preacher and delivering that. Preaching is the art of the man giving himself to the throng by means of voice and gesture and face and brains and heart, and the background of all these, himself."[7] The sermon is a shadow; the substance is the pastor. So if you're a pastor, you must take care of yourself both physically and emotionally.

It's All about Faithfulness!

As a pastor, it can be easy to get caught up in measuring success by numbers. How many people are in your congregation? How much money is coming in? But the truth is, success in ministry is not measured by numbers or prestige but by faithfulness to God. Dr. Vance Havner is instructive when he says, "None of these modern marks of ministerial success that measure the preacher by the statistics he can report were distinguishing characteristics in the Bible days." He goes on to say, "The final records may show some humble country preachers to have been just as Spirit-filled and blessed by God as another who moved multitudes. . . . We forget that God has a work for each man. . . . The itch for bigness is a dangerous thing." Don't let fame and figures be your goal, but faithfulness to God.[8]

It's okay to feel discouraged about the numbers. It's normal to feel like you're not doing enough. But please don't forget that your value is not based on numbers or outward appearances. You are valuable because you are faithfully serving the One who loves you. Pastor, find joy in your faithfulness. Rejoice that you are called to shepherd the people God has entrusted to you. Learn to rejoice in your faithfulness regardless of how large or small your congregation may be. Think about it—what will happen if your church never grows or never turns around, not slowly, not ever? Could you still find joy in your faithfulness to God?

7. Quayle and Wiersbe, *Pastor-Preacher*, 318–19.
8. Havner, *Peace Like a River*, loc. 208–20.

You Are Not Sisyphus!

Sisyphus was condemned to roll a boulder up a hill, only to have it roll back down again as soon as he reached the top. This punishment is said to represent the futility of all human effort. Unfortunately, for pastors, this analogy rings all too true. It's easy to feel like your work is never done as a pastor. There are always new challenges to face, and it often feels like you are pushing a boulder up a hill with no end in sight. But despite these difficulties, pastors should never lose heart. Here's why:

> Ours is not the unrequited toil of Sisyphus rolling uphill a stone which will rebound upon us. We are laboring for eternity, and we count not our work by each day's advance, as men measure theirs; it is God's work and must be measured by His standard. Be ye well assured that when time, and things created, and all that oppose themselves to the Lord's truth, shall be gone, every earnest sermon preached, and every importunate prayer offered, and every form of Christian service honestly rendered, shall remain embedded in the mighty structure which God from all eternity has resolved to raise to His own honor.[9]

It's not always easy to stand up in front of the same group of people and preach the gospel week after week, especially when it feels like no one is listening. You pour your heart and soul into ministering to your congregation. Yet, the congregation does not seem to be growing. It can be discouraging to see empty seats in the pews, feel like you're not reaching anyone, and wonder why you're even doing this.

Don't lose heart, pastor. You are not Sisyphus. Your work is not in vain. God is always at work, even when we can't see it. He is using your faithful preaching and teaching to change lives—even if those changes aren't immediately perceptible. You are laboring for eternity! You may never see the fruit of your labor while on this earth, but that doesn't mean it isn't worth it. So

---

9. Spurgeon, *All-Round Ministry*, 24.

keep pushing on, dear pastor—your faithful perseverance is not going unnoticed by the Almighty.

After our best Sunday, when our flock packs the pews, we exhibit clarity, concision, and conviction of speech; the Holy Spirit draws souls to himself through the gospel call to all. We see him tug through the word on our souls, effecting repentance and faith. People bow in submission and trust and give glory to Jesus! After that Sunday, we do it all over again. Then there is the Sunday when no one is there. You are preaching to a blinking dot on a camera, anticipating anyone is on the other end. You're prepared as always. God is present. He is always, but there seems to be a hollowness in the room. You hear your voice echo off the walls. What you would give for another mundane go-through-the-motions Sunday when people stared back at you with a blank face. Now you preach the same glorious gospel truth, and there is not a saint in sight to nod and offer a hearty amen in agreement. Nevertheless, it is the truth. And after the stream is over, you must rejoice in the same faithfulness you exhibited today as you did on your best Sunday and then do it all over again.

When asked, "How would you advise pastors to prepare themselves for preaching stress?" one research participant answered, "Expect it. Don't be surprised or oblivious to it. Keep your relationship with God vibrant and connected. This is the lifeline for your content in preaching." Pastor, I invite you to join me in recommitting ourselves to him. The work of the ministry is difficult and often thankless, but it is also one of immense privilege. We must never lose sight of being called to share the good news of Jesus Christ with the world. It is an honor to serve Christ this way. Let us take heart, knowing that God is with us. May God bless you in your work. Amen.

For free resources and articles to help churches help pastors preach well, visit preachwell.com.

Bibliography

"38% of U.S. Pastors Have Thought about Quitting Full-Time Ministry in the Past Year." Barna, Nov 16, 2021. https://www.barna.com/research/pastors-well-being/.

"Acute Mental Illness and Christian Faith Research Report." LifeWay Research, Sep 2014. http://lifewayresearch.com/wp-content/uploads/2014/09/Acute-Mental-Illness-and-Christian-Faith-Research-Report-1.pdf.

Adams, Harry Baker. *Preaching: The Burden and the Joy.* St. Louis: Chalice, 1996.

Adams, Jay E. *Preaching with Purpose: The Urgent Task of Homiletics.* Grand Rapids: Zondervan, 2015.

Allen, Jason K. *Portraits of a Pastor.* Chicago: Moody, 2017.

Anderson, Robert C. *The Effective Pastor.* Chicago: Moody, 1998.

Bailey, Sarah Pulliam. "'I Feel So Distant from God': Popular D.C.-Area Pastor Confesses He's Tired, Announces Sabbatical." *Washington Post,* Dec 11, 2019. https://www.washingtonpost.com/religion/2019/12/11/i-feel-so-distant-god-popular-dc-area-pastor-confesses-hes-tired-announces-sabbatical/.

Beecher, Henry Ward. *Popular Lectures on Preaching.* Glasgow: John S. Marr & Sons, 1872. http://archive.org/details/popularlectures00beecgoog

Beeke, Joel R., and Nicholas J. Thompson. *Pastors and Their Critics: A Guide to Coping with Criticism in the Ministry.* Phillipsburg, NJ: P&R, 2020.

Belleville, Linda. *Commentary on 1 Timothy.* Carol Stream, IL: Tyndale House, 2009.

Berry, Amanda, et al. "Ministry and Stress: Listening to Anglican Clergy in Wales." *Pastoral Psychology* 61.2 (Sep 2011) 165–78. https://doi.org/10.1007/s11089-011-0388-x.

Birk, Janice M., et al. "Religious Occupations and Stress Questionnaire (ROS): Instrument Development." *Counseling and Values* 45.2 (Jan 2001) 136–44. https://doi.org/10.1002/j.2161-007x.2001.tb00191.x.

Bounds, Edward M. *The Essential Works of E. M. Bounds.* Louisville: GLH, 2017. Kindle ed.

Briggs, Megan. "Why Are Pastors Depressed? A Look at the Research." ChurchLeaders, Sep 23, 2019. https://churchleaders.com/news/359562 -why-are-pastors-depressed-a-look-at-the-research.html.

Broadus, John A. *On the Preparation and Delivery of Sermons.* New York: HarperCollins, 2001.

Brosend, William. *Preaching Truth in the Age of Alternative Facts.* Nashville: Abingdon, 2018. Kindle ed.

Brown, Peter. *Augustine of Hippo: A Biography.* Berkeley, CA: University of California Press, 2013.

Brunson, Mac, and James W. Bryant. *The New Guidebook for Pastors.* Nashville: B&H, 2014.

Buice, Josh. "Legacy of Faithfulness: John Knox." G3 Ministries, Dec 3, 2015. https://g3min.org/legacy-of-faithfulness-john-knox/#:~:text=I%20 have%20never%20once%20feared,the%20face%20of%20the%20earth.

Capps, Donald. *Young Clergy: A Biographical-Developmental Study.* Binghamton, NY: Haworth Pastoral, 2005.

Carr, Caleb T., et al. "As Social Support: Relational Closeness, Automaticity, and Interpreting Social Support from Paralinguistic Digital Affordances in Social Media." *Computers in Human Behavior* 62 (Sep 2016) 385–93. https://doi.org/10.1016/j.chb.2016.03.087.

Carson, D. A. *For the Love of God: A Daily Companion for Discovering the Riches of God's Word.* Vol. 2. Nottingham: Inter-Varsity, 1998.

Carson, D. A., and John D. Woodbridge. *Letters Along the Way: A Novel of the Christian Life.* Wheaton, IL: Crossway, 1993.

Chandler, Diana. "Pastors Express 'Decision Fatigue', 'Ministerial Frustration' as COVID-19 Pandemic Lingers." Baptist Press, Jan 25, 2021. https:// www.baptistpress.com/resource-library/news/pastors-express-decision- fatigue-ministerial-frustration-as-covid-19-pandemic-lingers/.

Chapell, Bryan. *Christ-Centered Preaching: Redeeming the Expository Sermon.* Grand Rapids: Baker Academic, 2018.

Charles, H. B., Jr. "A Crash Course in Church Membership." H. B. Charles Jr., Aug 10, 2019. https://hbcharlesjr.com/resource-library/sermon-outlines/ a-crash-course-in-church-membership-1-thessalonians-512-15/.

Clinton, M. E., et al. "'It's Tough Hanging-Up a Call': The Relationships between Calling and Work Hours, Psychological Detachment, Sleep Quality, and Morning Vigor." *Journal of Occupational Health Psychology* 22.1 (2017) 28–39. https://doi.org/https://doi.org/10.1037/ocp0000025.

Covey, Stephen. *The 7 Habits of Highly Effective People.* London: Simon & Schuster, 1999.

Craddock, Fred B. *Preaching.* Nashville: Abingdon, 2010.

Croft, Brian. *Visit the Sick: Ministering God's Grace in Times of Illness.* Grand Rapids: Zondervan, 2014.

Daniel, Lillian, and Martin B. Copenhaver. *This Odd and Wondrous Calling: The Public and Private Lives of Two Ministers.* Grand Rapids: Eerdmans, 2009. Kindle ed.

Fabarez, Michael. *Preaching that Changes Lives.* Eugene, OR: Wipf & Stock, 2005.

Faulkner, Brooks R. *Burnout in Ministry.* Nashville: Broadman, 1981.

Francis, Leslie J., and Susan H. Jones. *Psychological Perspectives on Christian Ministry: A Reader.* Leominster, MA: Gracewing, 1996.

Godin, Seth. "Priorities." *Seth's Blog* (blog), Jan 3, 2020. https://seths. blog/2020/01/priorities/#:~:text=It%E2%80%99s%20comforting%20 to%20use%20someone%20else%E2%80%99s%20priorities%20 to,work%20is%20to%20own%20the%20priorities%20as%20well.

Green, Lisa Cannon. "Despite Stresses, Few Pastors Give Up on Ministry." Lifeway Research, Sep 1, 2015. https://research.lifeway.com/2015/09/01/despite -stresses-few-pastors-give-up-on-ministry/.

Gurnall, William. *The Christian in Complete Armour.* Louisville: GLH, 2021. Kindle ed.

Hart, Archibald D. "Depressed, Stressed, and Burned Out: What's Going on in My Life?" *Enrichment* 11.3 (Jul 2006) 20–30. https://enrichmentjournal. ag.org/-/media/Enrichment/Issue-PDFs/2006/EJ_2006_03_Summer.pdf.

———. *Unmasking Male Depression: Recognizing the Root Cause to Many Problem Behaviors such as Anger, Resentment, Abusiveness, Silence, Addictions, and Sexual Compulsiveness.* Nashville: Word, 2001.

Havner, Vance. *Peace Like a River: A Book of Meditations.* N.p.: Solid Christian, 1962. Kindle ed.

Hawkins, O. S. *High Calling High Anxiety.* Dallas: Anuity Board of the Southern Baptist Convention, 2003.

"'He Must Increase' Continues at Pastors' Conf." *Baptist Press*, Jun 16, 2015. https://www.baptistpress.com/resource-library/news/he-must-increase- continues-at-pastors-conf/.

Hiscox, Edward T., and Frank T. Hoadley. *The Star Book for Ministers.* 2nd rev. ed. Willow Grove, PA: Woodlawn Electronic, 1995.

Hughes, R. Kent, and Barbara Hughes. *Liberating Ministry from the Success Syndrome.* Wheaton, IL: Crossway, 2008. Kindle ed.

Jabusch, Willard Francis. *Person in the Pulpit.* Nashville: Abingdon, 1981.

Johnson, Jesse. "To Preach, to Really Preach . . ." The Cripplegate, Feb 28, 2012. https://thecripplegate.com/to-preach-to-really-preach/.

Keck, David. *Healthy Churches, Faithful Pastors: Covenant Expectations for Thriving Together.* Lanham, MD: Rowman & Littlefield, 2014.

Knowles, Michael P. *The Folly of Preaching: Models and Methods.* Grand Rapids: Eerdmans, 2007.

Larsen, David L. *The Anatomy of Preaching: Identifying the Issues in Preaching Today.* Grand Rapids: Kregel, 1999.

Lehmann, Helmut T., and Robert C. Schultz. *Luther's Works: Christian in Society III.* Vol. 46. Philadelphia: Fortress, 1967.

Lewis, Christopher Alan, et al. "Clergy Work-Related Psychological Health, Stress, and Burnout: An Introduction to this Special Issue of Mental Health, Religion and Culture." *Mental Health, Religion & Culture* 10.1 (Feb 13, 2007) 1–8. https://doi.org/10.1080/13674670601070541.

Lindholm, Greg, et al. "Clergy Wellness: An Assessment of Perceived Barriers to Achieving Healthier Lifestyles." *Journal of Religion and Health* 55.1 (Dec 25, 2014) 97–109. https://doi.org/10.1007/s10943-014-9976-2.

Lischer, Richard, and Willimon H. William, eds. *Concise Encyclopedia of Preaching*. Louisville: Westminster John Knox, 1995.

Lischer, Richard. *Theories of Preaching: Selected Readings in the Homiletical Tradition Paperback*. Durham, NC: The Labyrinth, 1987.

Lloyd-Jones, David Martyn. *Preaching and Preachers*. Grand Rapids: Zondervan, 2012.

———. *Spiritual Depression: Its Causes and Cures*. London: Pickering & Inglis, 1965.

London, H. B. *Pastors at Greater Risk*. Grand Rapids: Baker, 2012.

Long, Thomas G. *The Witness of Preaching*. Louisville: Westminster John Knox, 2016.

Luccock, Halford Edward. *In the Minister's Workshop*. Grand Rapids: Baker Book House, 1977.

Markquart, Edward F. *Quest for Better Preaching: Resources for Renewal in the Pulpit*. Minneapolis: Augsburg Fortress, 1985.

Massey, James Earl. *The Burdensome Joy of Preaching*. Nashville: Abingdon, 1998.

Mathis, David. "What Does a Good Sermon Cost? The Glad Sacrifice of Christian Preaching." Desiring God, Aug 16, 2018. https://www.desiringgod.org/articles/what-does-a-good-sermon-cost.

McClellan, Dave. *Preaching by Ear: Speaking God's Truth from the Inside Out*. Bellingham, WA: Lexham, 2014.

McDill, Wayne. *The 12 Essential Skills for Great Preaching*. Nashville: B&H, 2018. Kindle ed.

McIntosh, Gary, and Robert L. Edmondson. *It Only Hurts on Monday: Why Pastors Quit and What You Can Do about It*. Carol Stream, IL: ChurchSmart Resources, 1998.

McMinn, Mark R., et al. "Care for Pastors: Learning from Clergy and Their Spouses." *Pastoral Psychology* 53.6 (2005) 563–81. https://doi.org/10.1007/s11089-005-4821-y.

Meek, Katheryn Rhoads, et al. "Maintaining Personal Resiliency: Lessons Learned from Evangelical Protestant Clergy." *Journal of Psychology and Theology* 31.4 (2003) 339–47. https://doi.org/10.1177/009164710303100404.

Meisenhelder, Janice Bell, and Emily N. Chandler. "Frequency of Prayer and Functional Health in Presbyterian Pastors." *Journal for the Scientific Study of Religion* 40.2 (2001) 323–30. https://doi.org/10.1111/0021-8294.00059.

Meyer, F. B. *Expository Preaching Plans and Methods*. Toronto: The Upper Canada Tract Society, 1912.

Minirth, Frank B., and Paul D. Meier. *Happiness Is a Choice: New Ways to Enhance Joy and Meaning in Your Life*. Grand Rapids: Baker, 2013.

Monahan, Susanne C. "Who Controls Church Work? Organizational Effects on Jurisdictional Boundaries and Disputes in Churches." *Journal for the Scientific Study of Religion* 38.3 (Sep 1999) 370. https://doi.org/10.2307/1387758.

Morgan, G. Campbell. *The Practice of Prayer.* Chicago: Fleming H. Revell, 1906.

Morgenthaler, Sally. "Does Ministry Fuel Addictive Behavior?" *Leadership Journal* 27 (Winter 2006). https://www.christianitytoday.com/pastors/2006/winter/24.58.html.

Muck, Terry, and Paul Robbins. "The Sweet Torture of Sunday Morning." *Leadership Journal,* 2 (Summer 1981). https://www.christianitytoday.com/pastors/1981/summer/81l3016.html.

Nettles, Tom J. *Living by Revealed Truth: The Life and Pastoral Theology of Charles Haddon Spurgeon.* Ross-shire, Scotland: Mentor, 2013. Kindle ed.

Norman, Steve. *The Preacher as Sermon: How Who You Are Shapes What They Hear.* Carol Stream, IL: Christianity Today, 2021.

Owen, John. *The True Nature of a Gospel Church and Its Government.* London: Forgotten Books, 2018. Kindle ed. Orig. pub. 1689.

Pargament, Kenneth I., and Annette Mahoney. "Sacred Matters: Sanctification as a Vital Topic for the Psychology of Religion." *International Journal for the Psychology of Religion* 15.3 (2005) 179–98. https://doi.org/10.1207/s15327582ijpr1503_1.

Perkins, William. *The Art of Faithful Preaching.* Coconut Creek, FL: Puritan, 2012. Kindle ed.

Peterson, Eugene H. *Working the Angles: The Shape of Pastoral Integrity.* Grand Rapids: Eerdmans, 2001. Kindle ed.

Piper, John. *Brothers, We Are Not Professionals.* Nashville: B&H, 2013.

———. *Expository Exultation: Christian Preaching as Worship.* Wheaton: Crossway, 2018.

Prime, Derek J., and Alistair Begg. *On Being a Pastor.* Chicago: Moody, 2006.

Prior, Ryan. "Burnout Is an Official Medical Diagnosis, World Health Organization Says." *CNN,* May 27, 2019. https://www.cnn.com/2019/05/27/health/who-burnout-disease-trnd/index.html.

Proeschold-Bell, Rae Jean, and Jason Byassee. *Faithful and Fractured: Responding to the Clergy Health Crisis.* Grand Rapids: Baker Academic, 2018.

Proeschold-Bell, Rae Jean, et al. "The Glory of God Is a Human Being Fully Alive: Predictors of Positive Versus Negative Mental Health among Clergy." *Journal for the Scientific Study of Religion* 54.4 (2015) 702–21. https://doi.org/10.1111/jssr.12234.

Proeschold-Bell, Rae Jean, et al. "A Theoretical Model of the Holistic Health of United Methodist Clergy." *Journal of Religion and Health* 50.3 (2009) 700–720. https://doi.org/10.1007/s10943-009-9250-1.

Proeschold-Bell, Rae Jean, et al. "Use of a Randomized Multiple Baseline Design: Rationale and Design of the Spirited Life Holistic Health Intervention Study." *Contemporary Clinical Trials* 35.2 (Jul 2013) 138–52. https://doi.org/10.1016/j.cct.2013.05.005.

Proeschold-Bell, Rae Jean, et al. "Using Effort-Reward Imbalance Theory to Understand High Rates of Depression and Anxiety among Clergy." *The Journal of Primary Prevention* 34.6 (2013) 439–53. https://doi.org/10.1007/s10935-013-0321-4.

"The Pulpit's Personal Side." *Leadership Journal* 11 (Spring 1990). https://www.christianitytoday.com/pastors/1990/spring/90l2016.html.

Quayle, William A., and Warren W. Wiersbe. *The Pastor-Preacher*. Grand Rapids: Baker, 1979.

Quicke, Michael J. *360-Degree Preaching: Hearing, Speaking, and Living the Word*. Grand Rapids: Baker Academic, 2003. Kindle ed.

Rainer, Thom S. *High Expectations*. Nashville: Broadman & Holman, 1999. Kindle ed.

———. "How Much Time Do Pastors Spend Preparing a Sermon?" Church Answers, Feb 7, 2020. https://churchanswers.com/blog/how-much-time-do-pastors-spend-preparing-a-sermon/.

Ravenhill, Leonard. *America Is Too Young to Die*. Minneapolis: Bethany Fellowship, 1979.

Rummage, Stephen Nelson. *Planning Your Preaching: A Step-by-Step Guide for Developing a One-Year Preaching Calendar*. Grand Rapids: Kregel, 2002. Kindle ed.

Simpson, Matthew. "Lectures on Preaching Delivered to the Students of Yale College." N.p: R. D. Dickinson, 1879. http://archive.org/details/lecturesonpreaco1simpgoog.

Smietana, Bob. "For Some Pastors, the Past Year Was a Sign from God It Was Time to Quit." Religion News Service, May 7, 2021. https://religionnews.com/2021/05/07/for-some-pastors-the-past-year-was-a-sign-that-it-was-time-to-quit/.

Spaite, Daniel, and Debbie Salter Goodwin. *Time Bomb in the Church: Defusing Pastoral Burnout*. Kansas City: Beacon Hill, 1999.

Spurgeon, Charles H., et al. *Autobiography of Charles H. Spurgeon: Compiled from His Diary, Letters, and Records*. Whitefish, MT: Kessinger, 2007. Kindle ed.

Spurgeon, Charles H. *An All-Round Ministry*. London: Banner of Truth, 2018.

———. "The Burden of the Word of the Lord." In *The Metropolitan Tabernacle Pulpit* 35 (1889) 616. https://www.spurgeon.org/resource-library/sermons/the-burden-of-the-word-of-the-lord/#flipbook/.

———. "A Dire Disease Strangely Cured." In *The Metropolitan Tabernacle Pulpit: Sermons* 50. London: Passmore and Alabaster, 1904.

———. "For the Sick and the Afflicted." In *The Metropolitan Tabernacle Pulpit: Sermons* 22. London: Passmore & Alabaster, 1876.

———. *Lectures to My Students*. Grand Rapids: Zondervan, 2010.

———. *Only a Prayer Meeting: Forty Addresses at Metropolitan Tabernacle and Other Prayer-Meetings*. Bellingham, WA: Logos Bible Software, 2009.

———. "Removal." In *The Metropolitan Tabernacle Pulpit: Sermons* 48. London: Passmore and Alabaster, 1902.

———. "A Sermon of Personal Testimony." In *The Metropolitan Tabernacle Pulpit: Sermons* 44. London: Passmore and Alabaster, 1898.

———. "The Sure Triumph of the Crucified One." In *The Metropolitan Tabernacle Pulpit* 21 (1875) 241. https://www.spurgeon.org/resource-library/sermons/the-sure-triumph-of-the-crucified-one/#flipbook/.

Stetzer, Ed. *Christians in the Age of Outrage: How to Bring Our Best When the World Is at Its Worst.* Carol Stream, IL: Tyndale House, 2018.

Stott, John R. *Between Two Worlds.* Grand Rapids: Eerdmans, 1982.

"Studies from Louisiana State University Describe New Findings in Obesity (Occupational Conditions, Self-Care, and Obesity among Clergy in the United States)." *Obesity, Fitness & Wellness Week* (2015) 3362. https://link.gale.com/apps/doc/A401693174/AONE?u=anderson_cl&sid=AONE&xid=4c8114d4.

Vines, Jerry, and Jim L. Shaddix. *Progress in the Pulpit.* Chicago: Moody, 2017.

Warner, Janelle, and John D. Carter. "Loneliness, Marital Adjustment and Burnout in Pastoral and Lay Persons." *Journal of Psychology and Theology* 12.2 (1984) 125–31. https://doi.org/10.1177/009164718401200206.

Weiss, Donald H. *Managing Stress.* New York: American Management Association, 1987.

Wells, Carl R. "The Moderating Effects of Congregational and Denominational Support on the Impact of Stress on Clerical Emotional and Physical Health Status." *Pastoral Psychology,* 62 (2013) 873–88. https://doi.org/https://doi.org/10.1007/s11089-013-0522-z.

Wesley, John, and Alice Russie. *The Essential Works of John Wesley.* Uhrichsville, OH: Barbour, 2013.

"What Is Success in Ministry? How Can It Be Measured?" 9Marks, n.d. https://www.9marks.org/answer/what-success-ministry-how-can-it-be-measured/.

White, James Emery. *Meet Generation Z: Understanding and Reaching the New Post-Christian World.* Grand Rapids: Baker, 2017.

Wilkey, Lonnie. "TBMB Leader Discusses Pastoral Burnout." *Baptist and Reflector,* May 21, 2019. https://baptistandreflector.org/tbmb-leader-discusses-pastoral-burnout/.

Wilson, Michael Todd, and Brad Hoffmann. *Preventing Ministry Failure: A ShepherdCare Guide for Pastors, Ministers and Other Caregivers.* Downers Grove: InterVarsity, 2007.